1 *In*, *to*, & *is*

To parents/guardians: This is the first page of this workbook. Make sure your child looks at the page before beginning and completes each activity carefully. On this page, your child will practice tracing and identifying one sight word.

■ Look at the picture. Then trace and (say) the highlighted word.

in a box

in a box

in a box

in a tree

in a tree

in a tree

W0082041

A very good !s

■ Trace the path from the arrow (➡) to the star (★) following the word "in".

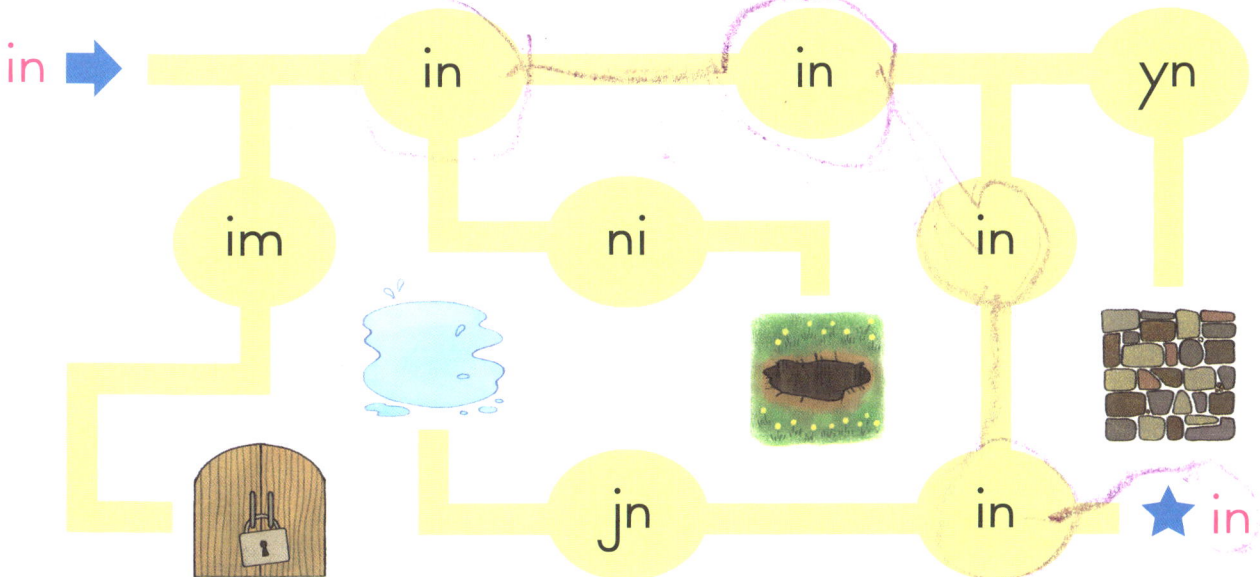

in ➡

in   in   yn

im   ni   in

jn   in   ★ in

1

To parents/guardians: It is important that your child say each sight word aloud. This will help strengthen their ability to recognize sight words while reading.

■ Look at the picture. Then trace and (say) the highlighted word.

to school

to school
to school

to sleep

to sleep
to sleep

■ Color each balloon that has the word "to". Use any color.

2 *In, to, & is*

To parents/guardians: In the second activity on this page, your child is asked to find the sight word in a word search puzzle. If they have difficulty with this activity, remind them to look across and down.

■ Look at the picture. Then trace and (say) the highlighted word.

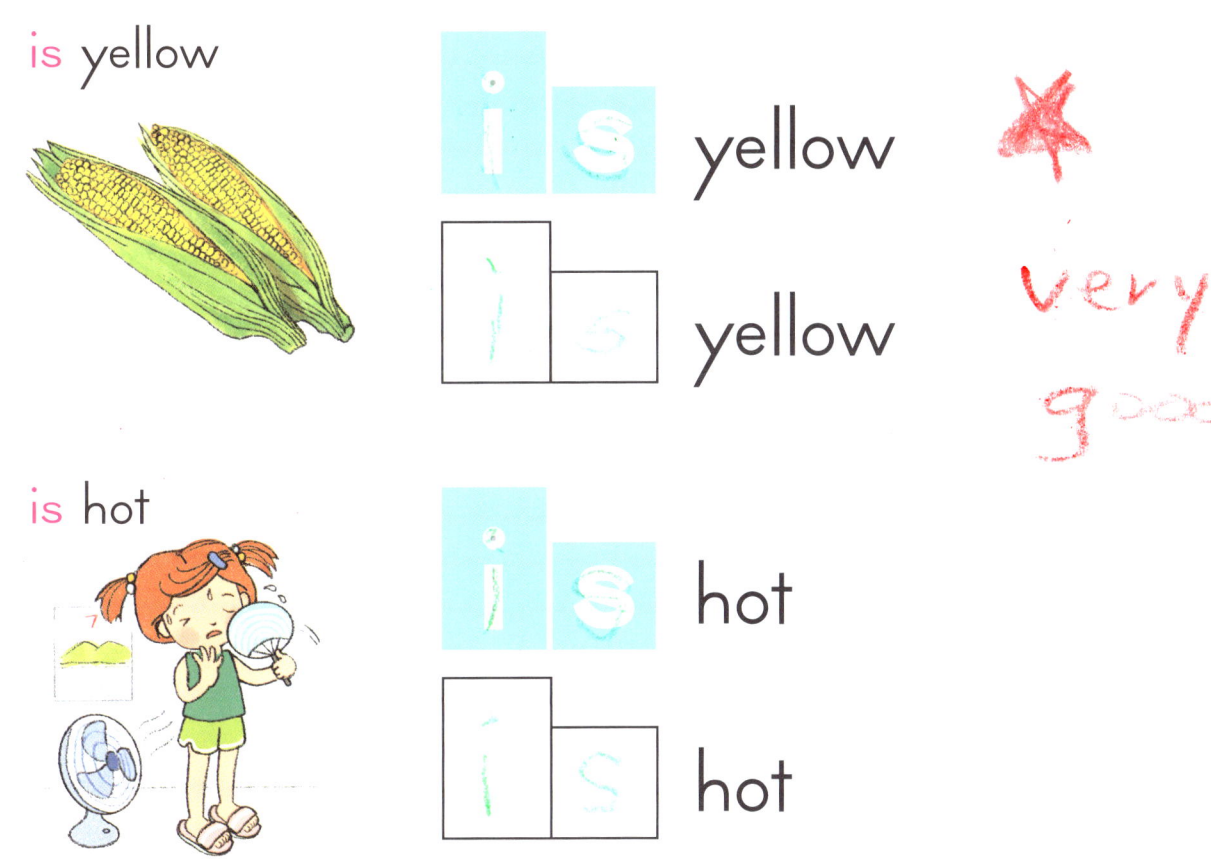

is yellow

i s yellow

i s yellow

very good

is hot

i s hot

i s hot

■ Find and circle the word "is". It appears **4** times. It may be written across (➡) or down (⬇).

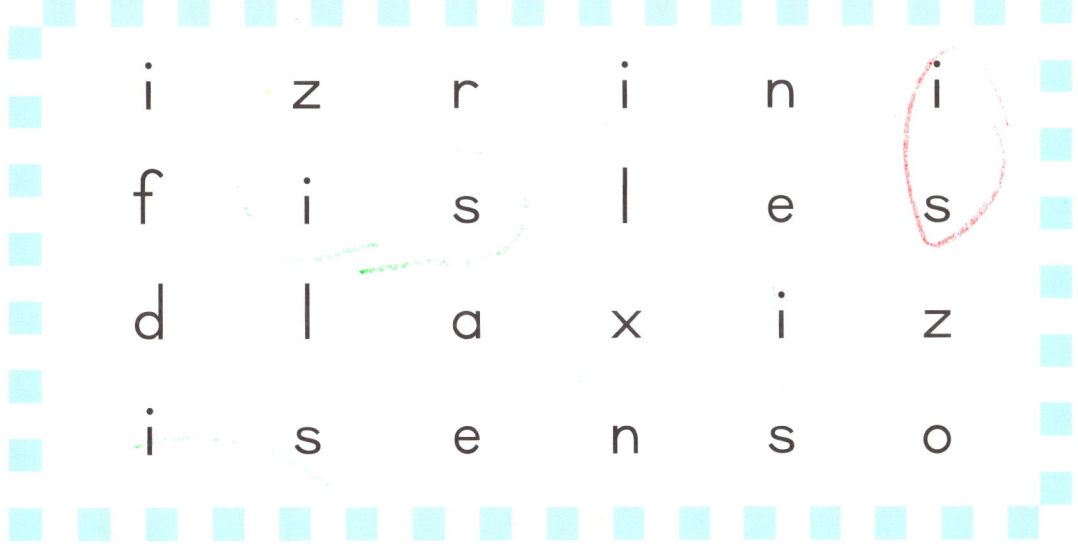

i z r i n i
f i s l e s
d l a x i z
i s e n s o

To parents/guardians: Here your child will practice writing the three sight words taught in this section. Your child can look at the pictures to help them understand the meaning of each sight word.

■ Look at the picture. Then trace and write the highlighted word.

in water

in water

i n water

to me

to me

t o me

is soft

i s soft

i s soft

Me, an, & we

So good!

Name

Date

/   /

To parents/guardians: In the maze activity on this page, your child will try to complete the maze by connecting the correctly spelled instances of the sight word. This activity will help your child learn to distinguish the sight word from other words or letter combinations that look or sound similar.

■ Look at the picture. Then trace and (say) the highlighted word.

play with me

play with

play with

give to me

give to

give to

■ Trace the path from the arrow (➡) to the star (★) following the word "me".

me ➡   mi       my

me   me   me

em      mc      me ★ me

Excellent !

■ Look at the picture. Then trace and (say) the highlighted word.

an apple

a n apple

a n apple

an egg

a n egg

a n egg

■ Color each flower that has the word "an". Use any color.

4

Me, an, & we

■ Look at the picture. Then trace and say the highlighted word.

we share

we bake

■ Find and circle the word "we". It appears **4** times. It may be written across (➡) or down (⬇).

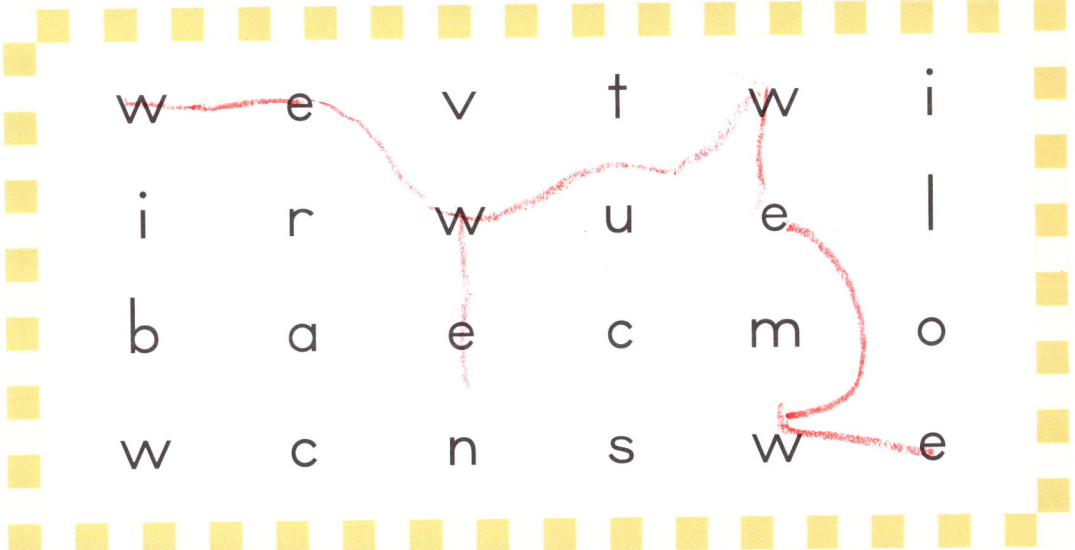

w e v t w i

i r w u e l

b a e c m o

w c n s w e

Awesome !

■ Look at the picture. Then trace and write the highlighted word.

my dad and me

my dad and

my dad and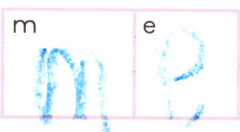

an owl

we won

 won

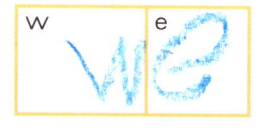 won

Review

In, to, is, me, an, & we

Name _____ Date ___ / ___

To parents/guardians: On this page, your child will review the six sight words taught in this section. If your child has difficulty, try first reading the words and phrases aloud with your child.

■ Trace each word. Then match each word with the phrase it is in. Part of the word is hidden.

in   is soft

to   in a box

is   to sleep

me   give to me

ap   we bake

we   an owl

✗ Really good!

To parents/guardians: This is the second review activity your child will complete in this book. Make sure your child says each word in the word bank aloud before filling in the blanks. Repeatedly saying the sight words aloud will help your child identify them.

■ (Say) each word in the word bank. Then fill in the blanks with words from the word bank.

| in | to | is | me | an | we |

| w | e | won |

| i | n | water |

play with | M | e |

| t | o | school |

| i | s | yellow |

| b | h | egg |

6 — By, up, & as

Perfect!

■ Look at the picture. Then trace and (say) the highlighted word.

by the water

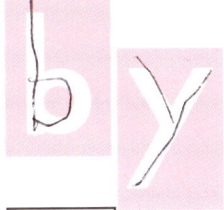 the water

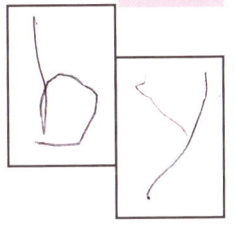 the water

by a fence

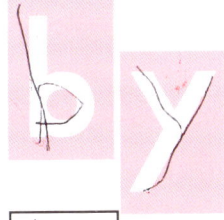 a fence

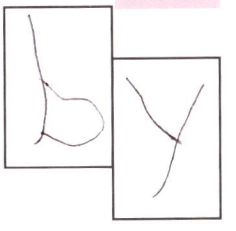 a fence

■ Trace the path from the arrow (➡) to the star (★) following the word "by".

by ➡   by   bg

   by   bi

bye

yb   by   by   ★ by

■ Look at the picture. Then trace and (say) the highlighted word.

look up

look **up**

look **up**

up the ladder

up the ladder

up the ladder

■ Color each crab that has the word "up". Use any color.

7 *By, up, & as*

To parents/guardians: Many sight words cannot be easily sounded out using basic phonics rules. Repeated practice will help your child learn to read these words without frustration.

■ Look at the picture. Then trace and (say) the highlighted word.

cold **as** ice

cold **a s** ice

cold ☐ ☐ ice

tall **as** a tree

tall **a s** a tree

tall ☐ ☐ a tree

■ Find and circle the word "**as**". It appears **4** times. It may be written across (➡) or down (⬇).

a	z	r	i	a	s
f	a	s	l	e	a
d	c	a	x	a	m
a	s	e	n	s	a

■ Look at the picture. Then trace and write the highlighted word.

by the flowers

the flowers

the flowers

up in the sky

in the sky

in the sky

slow as a snail

slow   a snail

slow   a snail

8

A, I, & it

To parents/guardians: In this section, your child will practice writing and identifying sight words that are also single letters. It is important to help your child recognize the difference betweena *a* as a vowel only and *a* used as a word.

■ Look at the picture. Then trace and (say) the highlighted word.

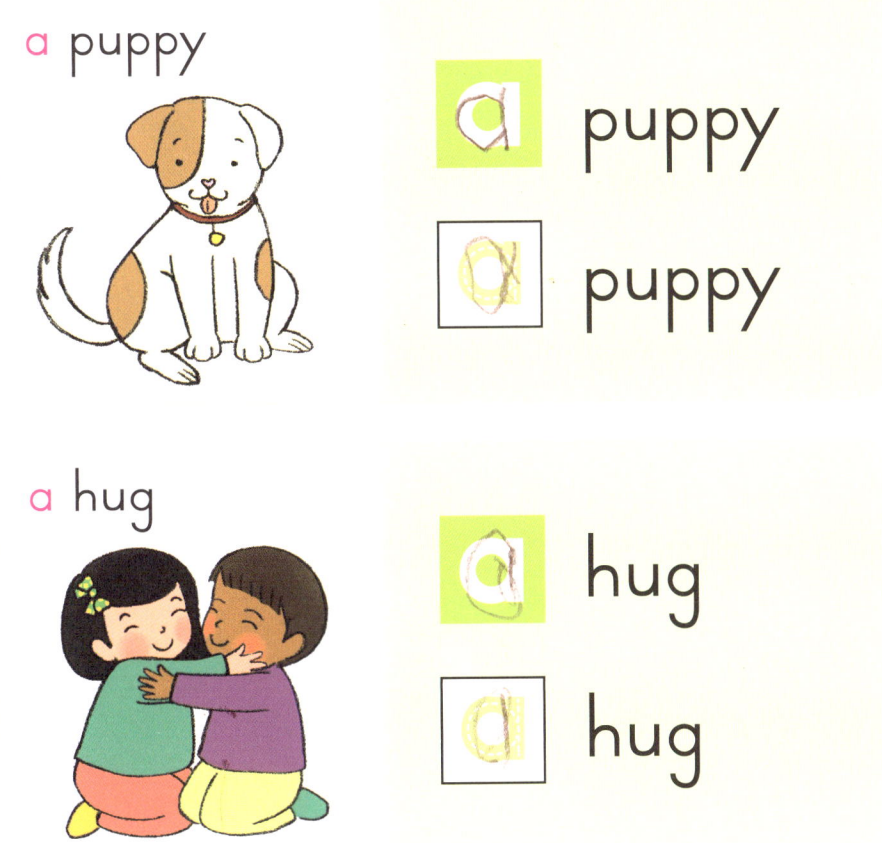

a puppy

a puppy

a puppy

a hug

a hug

a hug

■ Trace the path from the arrow (➡) to the star (★) following the word "a".

To parents/guardians: Here your child will practice writing and identifying *I* as a sight word. Point out to your child that *I* used by itself as a word is capitalized.

■ Look at the picture. Then trace and (say) the highlighted word.

I drive.

I drive.

I cook.

I cook.

■ Color each penguin that has the word "I". Use any color.

9   *A, I, & it*

- Look at the picture. Then trace and (say) the highlighted word.

paint it

paint

paint

hang it

hang

hang

- Find and circle the word "it". It appears **4** times. It may be written across (➡) or down (⬇).

i	t	r	j	i	t
f	i	i	t	e	f
d	l	s	y	i	t
t	i	n	e	s	y

■ Look at the picture. Then trace and write the highlighted word.

a star

a star

a star

I wave.

I wave.

I wave.

hear it

hear

hear

Review

By, up, as, a, I, & it

To parents/guardians: When reviewing multiple sight words on one page, it is important that your child correctly identify each one. If your child struggles with this activity, please go back and review the section for any word(s) your child has trouble with.

■ Trace each word. Then match each word with the phrase or sentence it is in. Part of the word is hidden.

 ●   ● by the water

 ●   ● cold a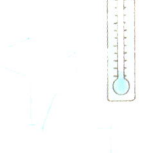s ice

 ●   ● up the ladder

 ●   ● hear it

 ●   ● a puppy

 ●   ● I wave.

■ (Say) each word in the word bank. Then fill in the blanks with words from the word bank.

| by | up | as | a | I | it |

□ hug

paint □□

□□ a fence

tall □□ a tree

□ in the sky

□ cook.

11

If, go, & do

To parents/guardians: Some sight words such as *if* and *it* can be hard to tell apart. Make sure your child correctly traces a path through the maze by only connecting correctly spelled instances of the word *if*.

■ Look at the picture. Then trace and (say) the highlighted word.

if it rains

if   it rains

☐☐   it rains

if she wins

if   she wins

☐☐   she wins

■ Trace the path from the arrow (➡) to the star (⭐) following the word "if".

if ➡   if   if

           ih

      fi   if

it   ip   if   ⭐ if

■ Look at the picture. Then trace and (say) the highlighted word.

go home

go home

go home

go outside

go outside

go outside

■ Color each balloon that has the word "go". Use any color.

If, go, & do

■ Look at the picture. Then trace and (say) the highlighted word.

do a flip

do a flip

a flip

do my job

do my job

my job

■ Find and circle the word "do". It appears **4** times. It may be written across (➡) or down (⬇).

d	v	b	j	d	o
u	d	o	e	u	s
e	u	c	a	d	c
d	o	p	b	o	u

■ Look at the picture. Then trace and write the highlighted word.

if it grows

it grows

it grows

go up

up

up

do not talk

not talk

not talk

On, at, & he

■ Look at the picture. Then trace and (say) the highlighted word.

on the rug

on the rug

☐☐ the rug

on a pillow

on a pillow

☐☐ a pillow

■ Trace the path from the arrow (➡) to the star (⭐) following the word "on".

■ Look at the picture. Then trace and (say) the highlighted word.

at school

at school

at school

at a party

at a party

at a party

■ Color each flower that has the word "at". Use any color.

On, at, & he

■ Look at the picture. Then trace and (say) the highlighted word.

he sits

he sits
he sits

he roars

he roars
he roars

■ Find and circle the word "he". It appears **4** times. It may be written across (➡) or down (⬇).

h	i	n	s	h	o
c	d	h	c	e	t
k	i	e	e	b	h
h	e	v	j	t	e

■ Look at the picture. Then trace and write the highlighted word.

on my chair

o n my chair

o n my chair

at the top

a t the top

a t the top

he reads

h e reads

h e reads

Review

If, go, do, on, at, & he

To parents/guardians: Reviewing six sight words on one page can be a challenging task for your child. Remind your child to use the pictures as clues and to say each word aloud.

■ Trace each word. Then match each word with the phrase it is in. Part of the word is hidden.

 go outside

 do a flip

 if it rains

 he roars

 on my chair

 at a party

■ (Say) each word in the word bank. Then fill in the blanks with words from the word bank.

if	go	do	on	at	he

the rug

school

up

my job

it grows

reads

My, am, & so

■ Look at the picture. Then trace and (say) the highlighted word.

my foot

my foot

◻◻ foot

my toy

my toy

◻◻ toy

■ Trace the path from the arrow (➡) to the star (★) following the
word "my".

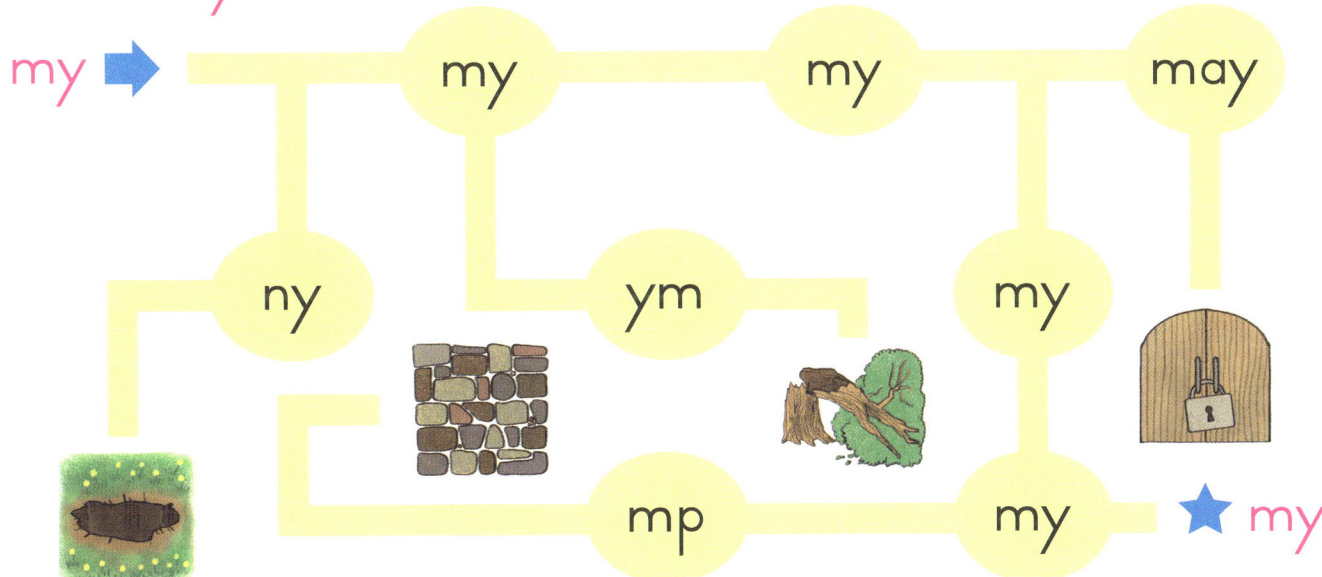

my ➡   my   my   may

ny   ym   my

mp   my   ★ my

■ Look at the picture. Then trace and (say) the highlighted word.

am happy

am happy

happy

am sad

am sad

sad

■ Color each crab that has the word "**am**". Use any color.

My, am, & so

To parents/guardians: Being able to recognize sight words instantaneously, without having to sound them out, will increase your child's reading speed and fluency.

■ Look at the picture. Then trace and (say) the highlighted word.

so happy

so happy

☐ happy

so sad

so sad

☐ sad

■ Find and circle the word "so". It appears **4** times. It may be written across (➡) or down (⬇).

o	s	o	a	s	o
v	u	z	o	p	u
s	c	b	s	z	o
o	h	n	o	t	w

■ Look at the picture. Then trace and write the highlighted word.

my sister

sister

| m | y |

sister

am sleepy

sleepy

| a | m |

sleepy

so sleepy

sleepy

| s | o |

sleepy

Or, of, & be

■ Look at the picture. Then trace and say the highlighted word.

red or blue

red **or** blue

red ☐☐ blue

fork or spoon

fork **or** spoon

fork ☐☐ spoon

■ Trace the path from the arrow (➡) to the star (★) following the word "or".

or ➡   our   

                                   ur

or   or   or

ore    ro   or   ★ or

■ Look at the picture. Then trace and (say) the highlighted word.

ball of yarn

ball **of** yarn

ball **of** yarn

bowl of soup

bowl **of** soup

bowl **of** soup

■ Color each penguin that has the word "of". Use any color.

Or, of, & be

■ Look at the picture. Then trace and (say) the highlighted word.

be like her

be like her

be like her

be friends

be friends

be friends

■ Find and circle the word "be". It appears **4** times. It may be written across (➡) or down (⬇).

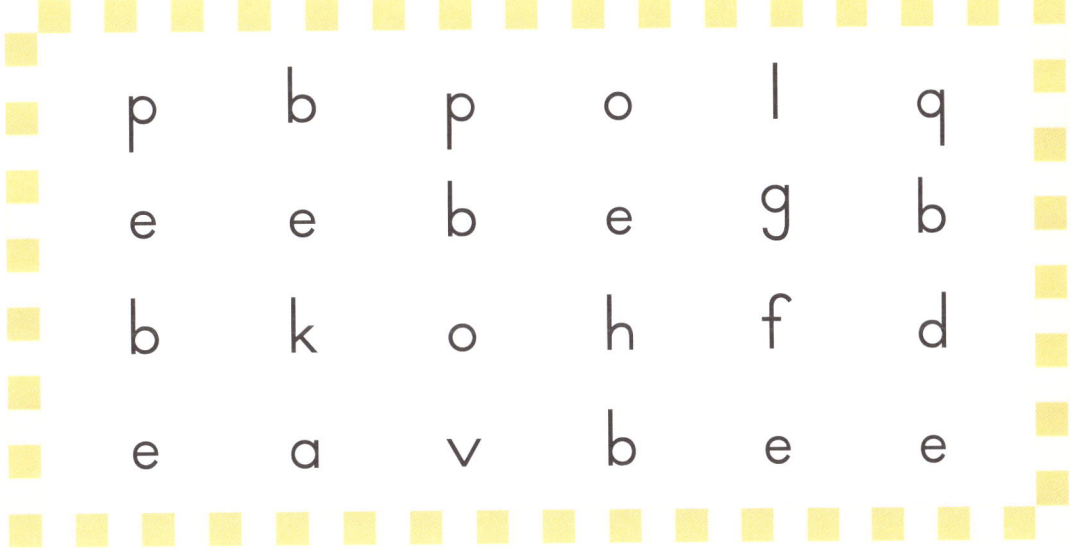

p	b	p	o	l	q
e	e	b	e	g	b
b	k	o	h	f	d
e	a	v	b	e	e

■ Look at the picture. Then trace and write the highlighted word.

draw or color

draw [   ] color

draw [o   r] color

bag of food

bag [o   f] food

bag [o   f] food

be brave

[b   e] brave

[b   e] brave

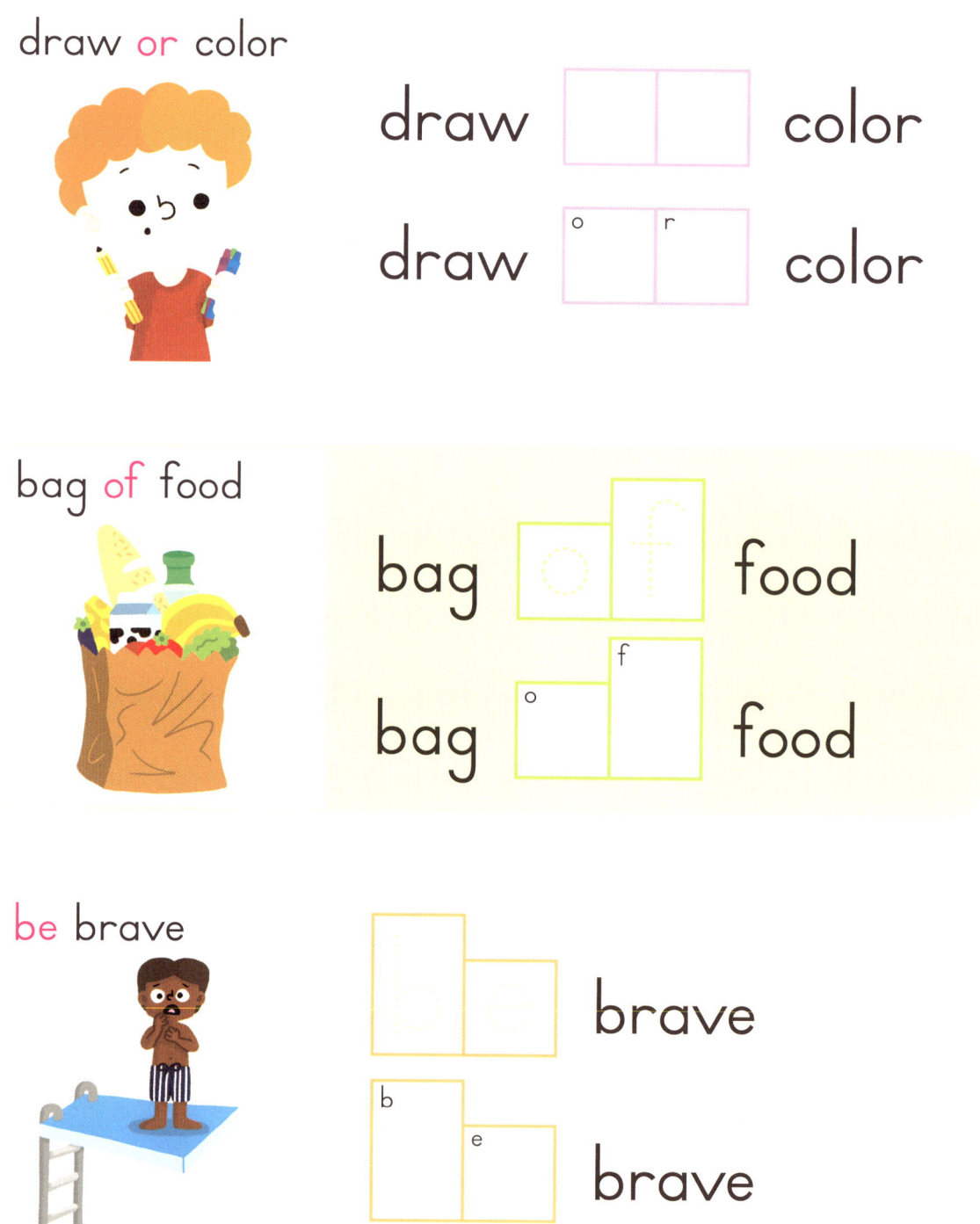

Review
My, am, so, or, of, & be

■ Trace each word. Then match each word with the phrase it is in. Part of the word is hidden.

am sad

my foot

so happy

be friends

fork or spoon

bowl of soup

To parents/guardians: If your child has trouble with this activity, suggest that they look at the shapes and sizes of the letter boxes. The boxes offer clues about which word goes with each phrase.

■ (Say) each word in the word bank. Then fill in the blanks with words from the word bank.

my	am	so	or	of	be

brave

red ☐ blue

toy

sleepy

sleepy

ball yarn

21 *See, not, & the*

Name   Date
                              /   /

To parents/guardians: The words in this book are generally organized by length. Now the words are three letters long. Longer words may be more difficult for your child to recognize and write. As words get longer, you may want to erase the completed activities and have your child repeat them for more practice.

■ Look at the picture. Then trace and (say) the highlighted word.

see me

see me

see a mouse

see a mouse

■ Trace the path from the arrow (➡) to the star (★) following the word "see".

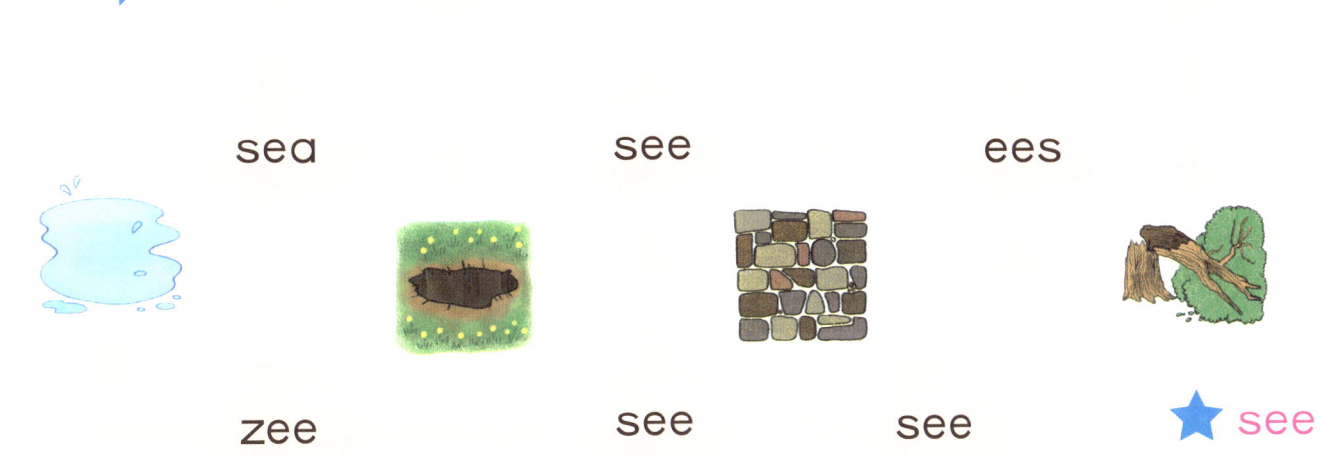

see ➡   see   se

sea   see   ees

zee   see   see   ★ see

■ Look at the picture. Then trace and (say) the highlighted word.

not raining

not raining

raining

not my shoe

not my shoe

my shoe

■ Color each balloon that has the word "not". Use any color.

See, *not*, & *the*

22

To parents/guardians: On this page, your child will learn the word *the*. *The* is difficult to sound out using basic phonics rules. Repeatedly seeing *the* and saying *the* aloud will help your child recognize it as they learn to read.

■ Look at the picture. Then trace and (say) the highlighted word.

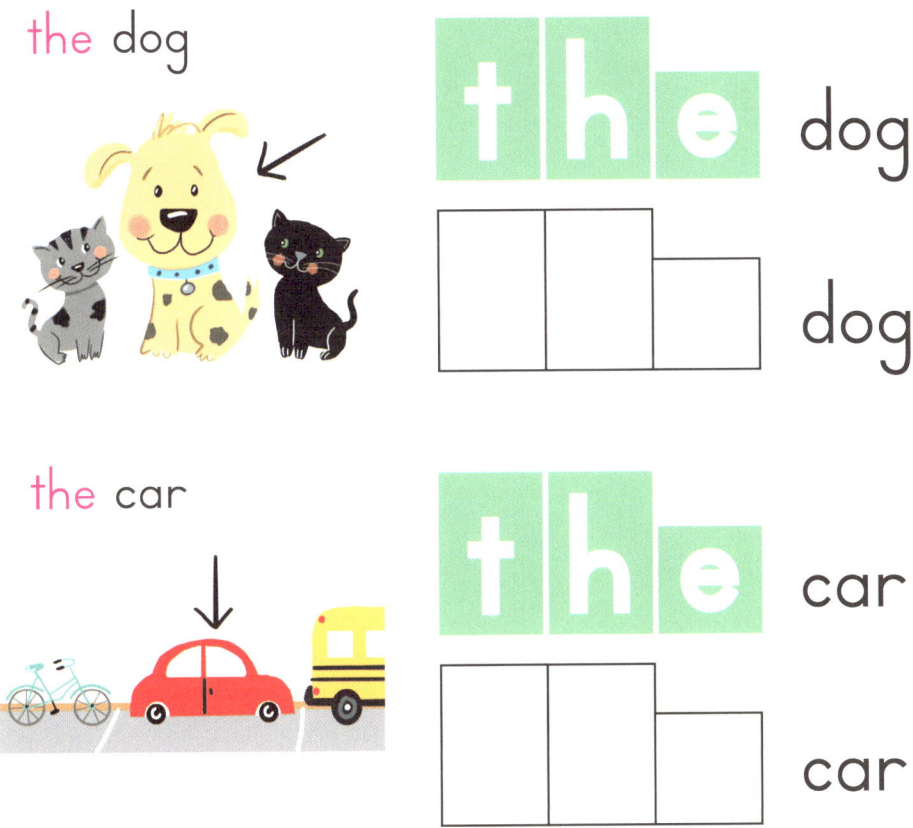

the dog

the car

■ Find and circle the word "the". It appears **4** times. It may be written across (➡) or down (⬇).

■ Look at the picture. Then trace and write the highlighted word.

see the bird

the bird

s	e	e

the bird

not hungry

hungry

n	o	t

hungry

the tree

tree

t	h	e

tree

23 And, for, & can

■ Look at the picture. Then trace and (say) the highlighted word.

socks and shoes

socks **and** shoes

socks and shoes

milk and cookies

milk **and** cookies

milk and cookies

■ Trace the path from the arrow (➡) to the star (⭐) following the word "and".

and ➡   add   and   and

              and   and   ann

any   nda   ⭐ and

45

■ Look at the picture. Then trace and (say) the highlighted word.

for you

for you

for you

for my brother

for my brother

for my brother

■ Color each flower that has the word "for". Use any color.

And, for, & can

■ Look at the picture. Then trace and (say) the highlighted word.

can walk

can walk

can play

can play

■ Find and circle the word "can". It appears **4** times. It may be written across (➡) or down (⬇).

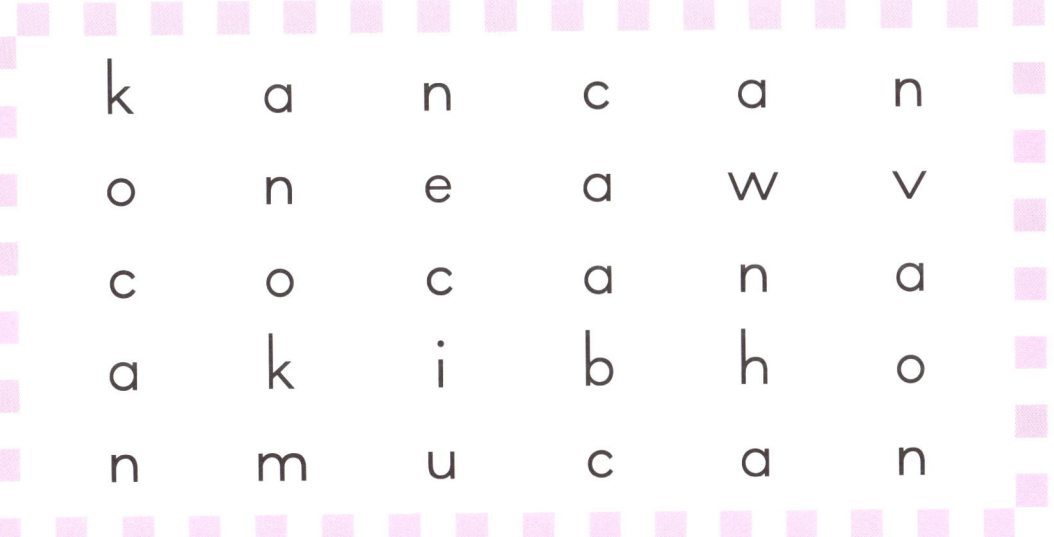

k	a	n	c	a	n
o	n	e	a	w	v
c	o	c	a	n	a
a	k	i	b	h	o
n	m	u	c	a	n

■ Look at the picture. Then trace and write the highlighted word.

green **and** yellow

green a n d yellow

green a n d yellow

for my dad

f o r my dad

f o r my dad

can write

write

c a n write

25 Review

See, not, the, and, for, & can

■ Trace each word. Then match each word with the phrase it is in. Part of the word is hidden.

  the car

 not raining

 see a mouse

 and

 can walk

 socks and shoes

 for you

■ (Say) each word in the word bank. Then fill in the blanks with words from the word bank.

see   not   the   and   for   can

hungry

dog

milk   cookies

me

write

my brother

26 *Him, her, & has*

■ Look at the picture. Then trace and (say) the highlighted word.

hug him

hug **him**

hug ☐☐☐

give him food

give **him** food

give ☐☐☐ food

■ Trace the path from the arrow (➡) to the star (⭐) following the word "him".

him ➡

him

him

hlm

hum   hymm

him

kim

him   ⭐ him

■ Look at the picture. Then trace and (say) the highlighted word.

her bat

her bat

her bat

her crown

her crown

her crown

■ Color each crab that has the word "her". Use any color.

Him, her, & has

■ Look at the picture. Then trace and (say) the highlighted word.

has a pet

has a pet
a pet
a pet

has a book

has a book
a book
a book

■ Find and circle the word "has". It appears **4** times. It may be written across (➡) or down (⬇).

h	u	s	p	o	h
a	y	h	a	h	a
s	h	a	s	z	s
w	i	s	f	o	n
e	z	x	h	a	s

■ Look at the picture. Then trace and write the highlighted word.

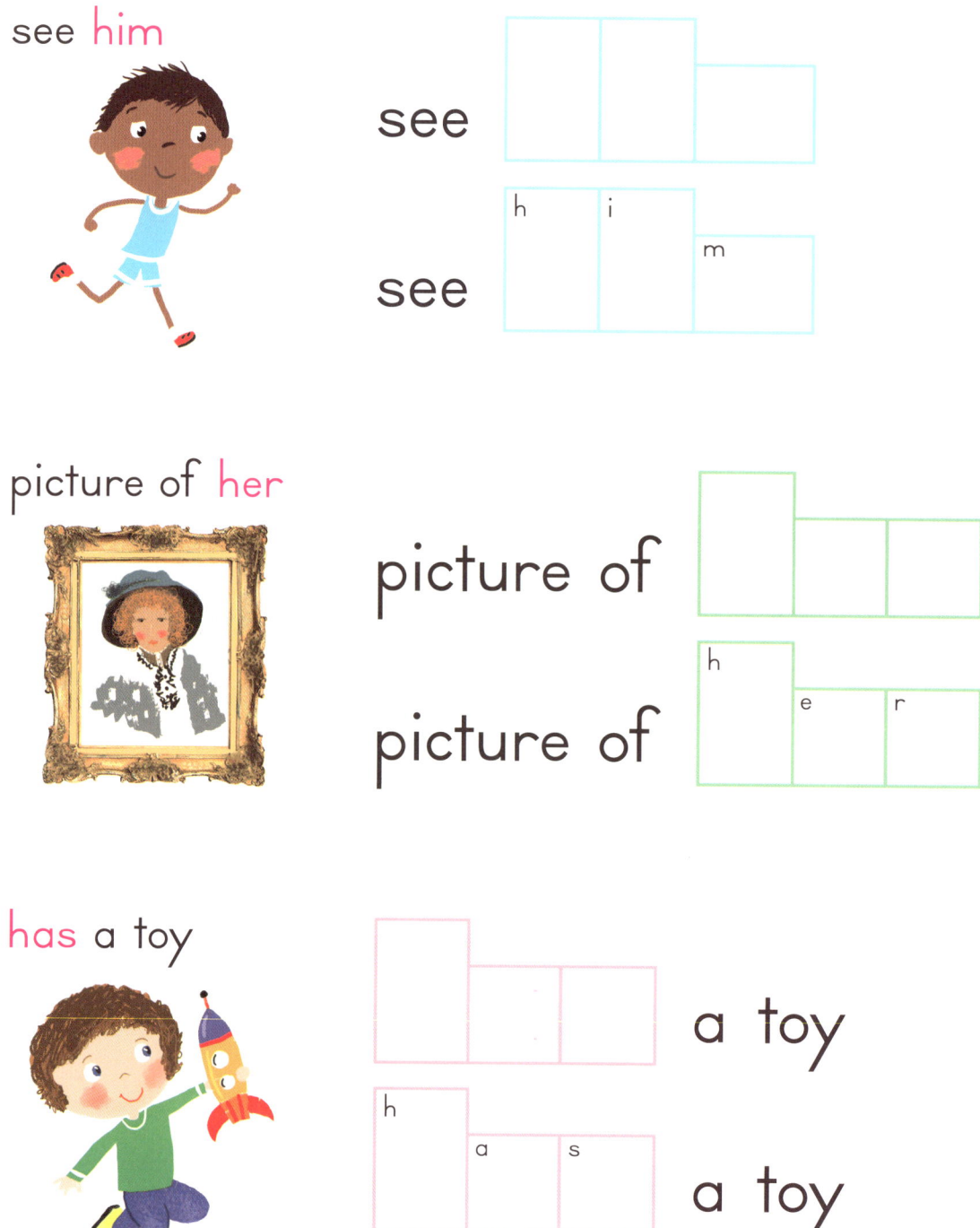

see him

see

see

picture of her

picture of

picture of

has a toy

a toy

a toy

28 You, was, & too

Name

Date

/   /

To parents/guardians: Your child might have trouble sounding out the word *you*. If your child needs help, you can say *you* aloud first and ask them to repeat after you.

■ Look at the picture. Then trace and (say) the highlighted word.

see you

see **you**

see you

you and me

you and me

you and me

■ Trace the path from the arrow (➡) to the star (⭐) following the word "you".

you ➡

yoo

you

yeo

you

you

you

ycu

yu

⭐ you

■ Look at the picture. Then trace and (say) the highlighted word.

was late

was late

			late

was lost

was lost

			lost

■ Color each penguin that has the word "was". Use any color.

You, was, & too

■ Look at the picture. Then trace and (say) the highlighted word.

too hot

t o o hot

t o o hot

too big

t o o big

t o o big

■ Find and circle the word "too". It appears **4** times. It may be written across (➡) or down (⬇).

t	o	o	c	p	t
o	h	v	d	u	o
t	r	e	o	f	o
o	t	o	o	i	s
o	u	f	t	w	o

■ Look at the picture. Then trace and write the highlighted word.

you won

y o u   won

y o u   won

was happy

happy

w a s   happy

too cold

t o o   cold

t o o   cold

Review

Him, her, has, you, was, & too

■ Trace each word. Then match each word with the phrase it is in. Part of the word is hidden.

■ (Say) each word in the word bank. Then fill in the blanks with words from the word bank.

him   her   has   you   was   too

bat

and me

a book

late

hot

give   food

31 *His, are, & but*

Date

/ /

■ Look at the picture. Then trace and (say) the highlighted word.

his nose

h i s nose

☐☐☐ nose

his tail

h i s tail

☐☐☐ tail

■ Trace the path from the arrow (➡) to the star (⭐) following the word "his".

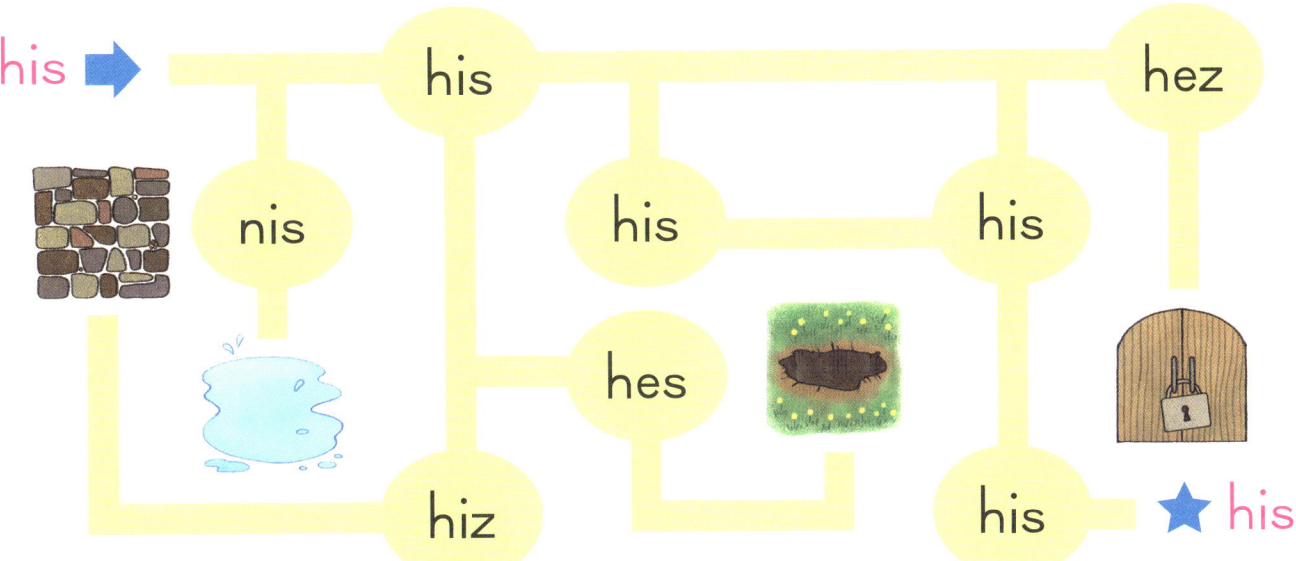

his ➡ his   hez

nis   his   his

hes

hiz   his   ⭐ his

61

■ Look at the picture. Then trace and (say) the highlighted word.

are green

are green

☐☐☐ green

are soft

are soft

☐☐☐ soft

■ Color each balloon that has the word "are". Use any color.

His, are, & but

Date

/   /

■ Look at the picture. Then trace and (say) the highlighted word.

cold **but** sunny

cold  sunny

cold ⬜⬜⬜ sunny

tired **but** happy

tired  happy

tired ⬜⬜⬜ happy

■ Find and circle the word "**but**". It appears **4** times. It may be written across (➡) or down (⬇).

t	i	b	o	p	u
w	b	u	l	b	c
b	u	t	l	u	s
o	f	a	b	t	f
t	b	u	t	n	n

■ Look at the picture. Then trace and write the highlighted word.

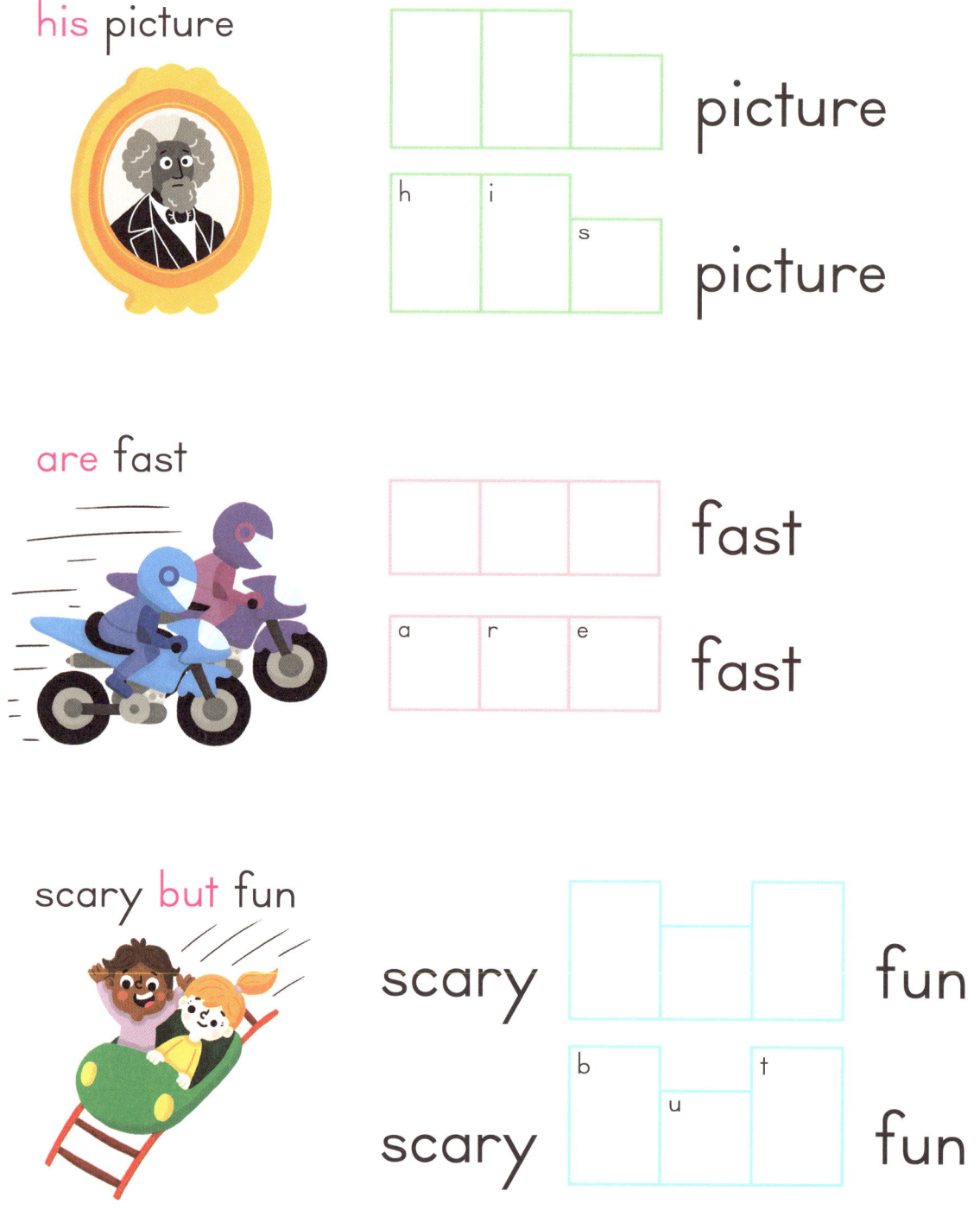

his picture

picture

| h | i | |
| | | s |

picture

are fast

fast

| a | r | e |

fast

scary but fun

scary   fun

| b | | t |
| | u | |

scary   fun

33 *Off, saw, & get*

■ Look at the picture. Then trace and (say) the highlighted word.

jump off

jump **off**

jump

take off

take **off**

take

■ Trace the path from the arrow (➡) to the star (★) following the word "off".

off ➡   ott   of

          off   off   off

                              off

uff   ffo   ★ off

■ Look at the picture. Then trace and (say) the highlighted word.

■ Color each flower that has the word "saw". Use any color.

34

Off, saw, & get

■ Look at the picture. Then trace and (say) the highlighted word.

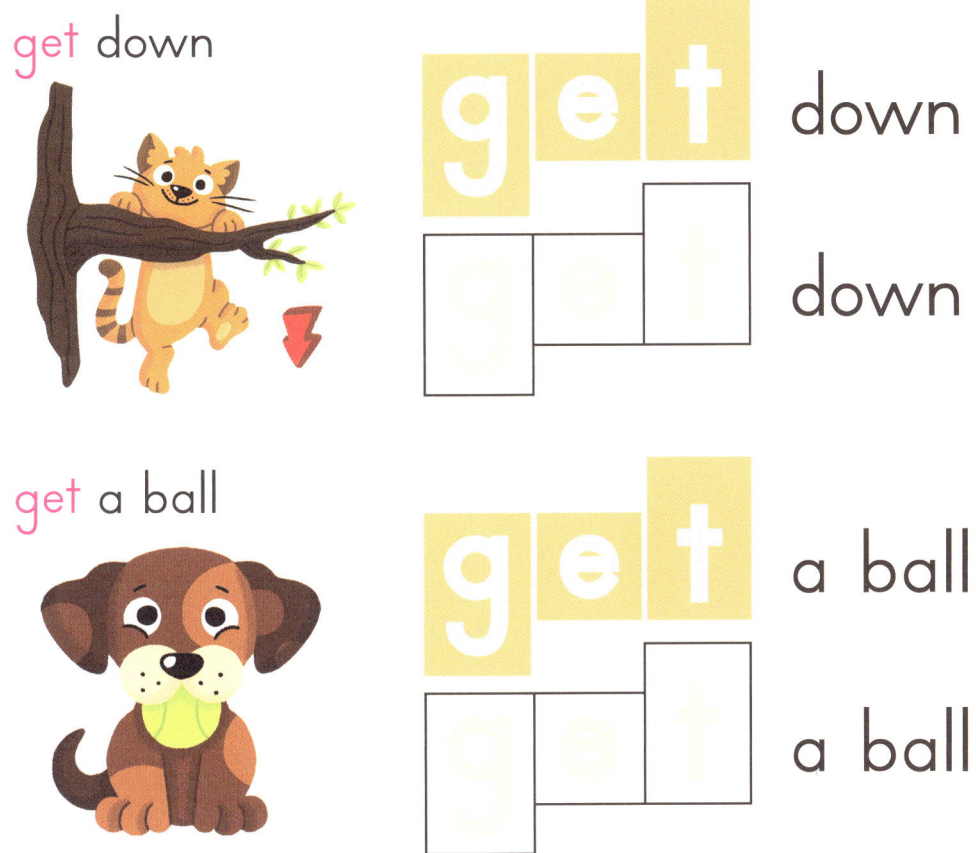

get down

get down
get down

get a ball

get a ball
get a ball

■ Find and circle the word "**get**". It appears **4** times. It may be written across (➡) or down (⬇).

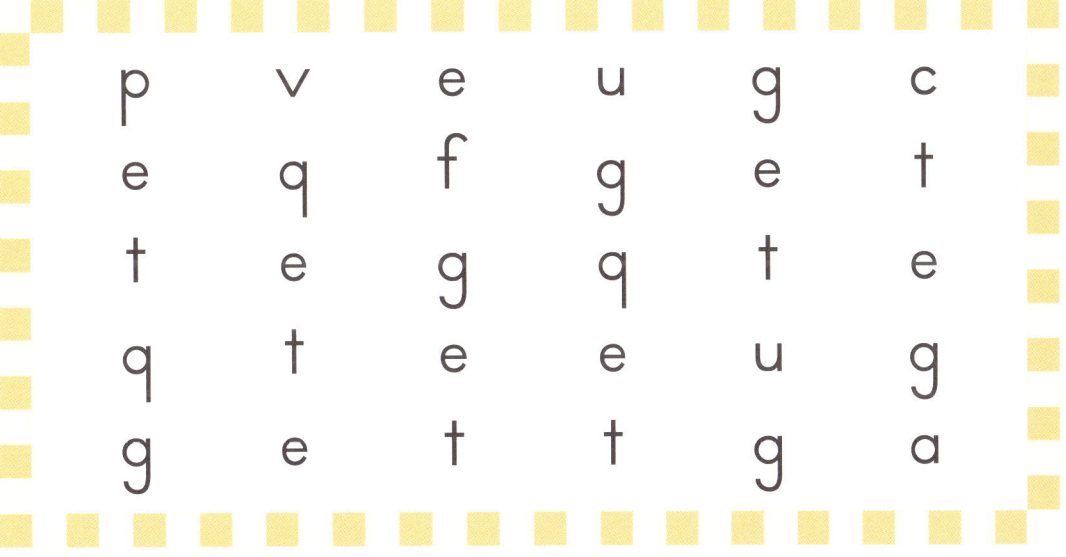

p	v	e	u	g	c
e	q	f	g	e	t
t	e	g	q	t	e
q	t	e	e	u	g
g	e	t	t	g	a

■ Look at the picture. Then trace and write the highlighted word.

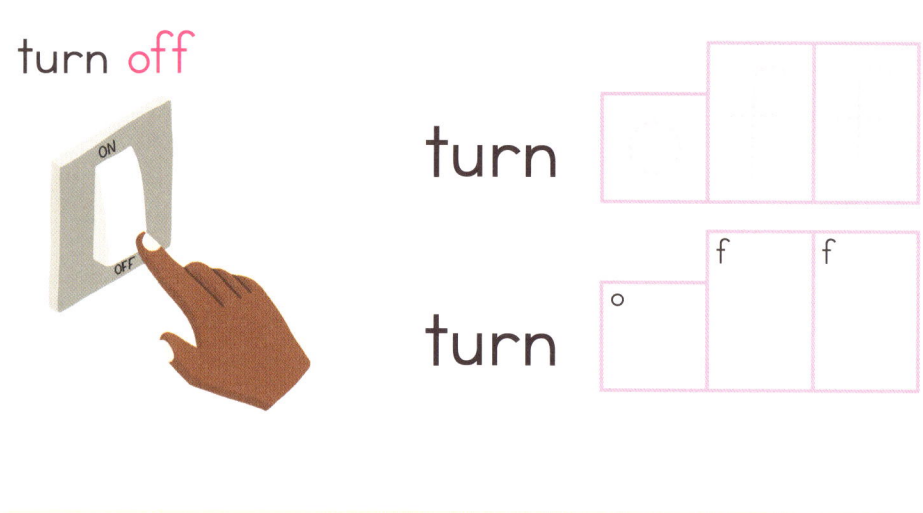

turn **off**

turn

turn

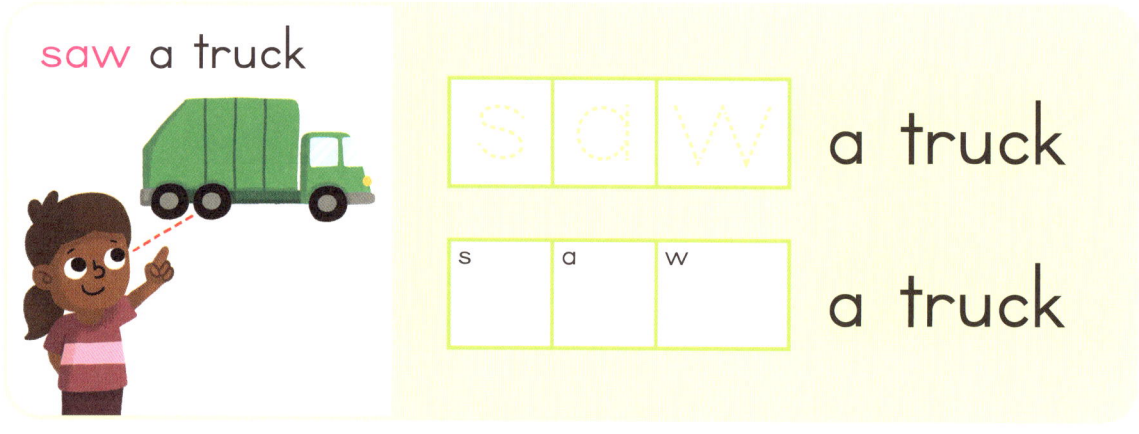

saw a truck

saw   a truck

s a w   a truck

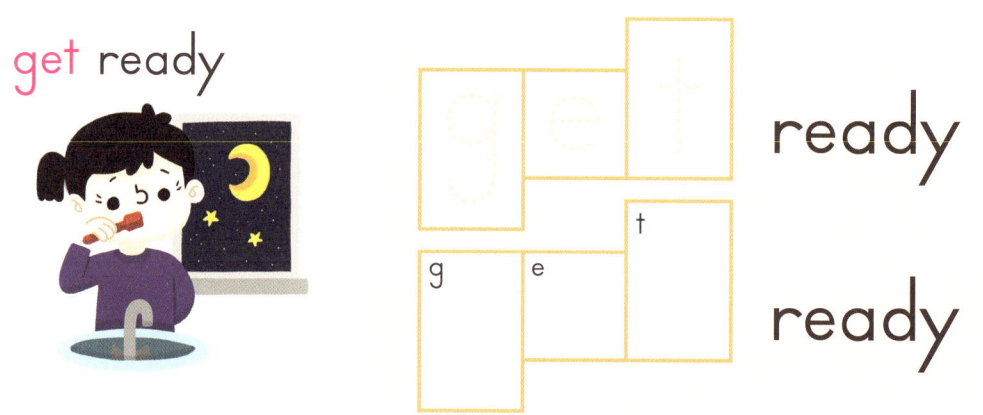

get ready

get   ready

g e t   ready

Review

35

His, are, but, off, saw, & get

■ Trace each word. Then match each word with the phrase it is in. Part of the word is hidden.

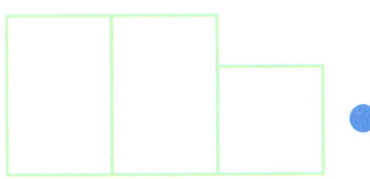 • • cold b**u**t sunny

 • • ar**e** soft

 • • hi**s** nose

 • • **s**aw a truck

 s a w • • jump of**f**

 • • g**e**t ready

■ (Say) each word in the word bank. Then fill in the blanks with words from the word bank.

| his | are | but | off | saw | get |

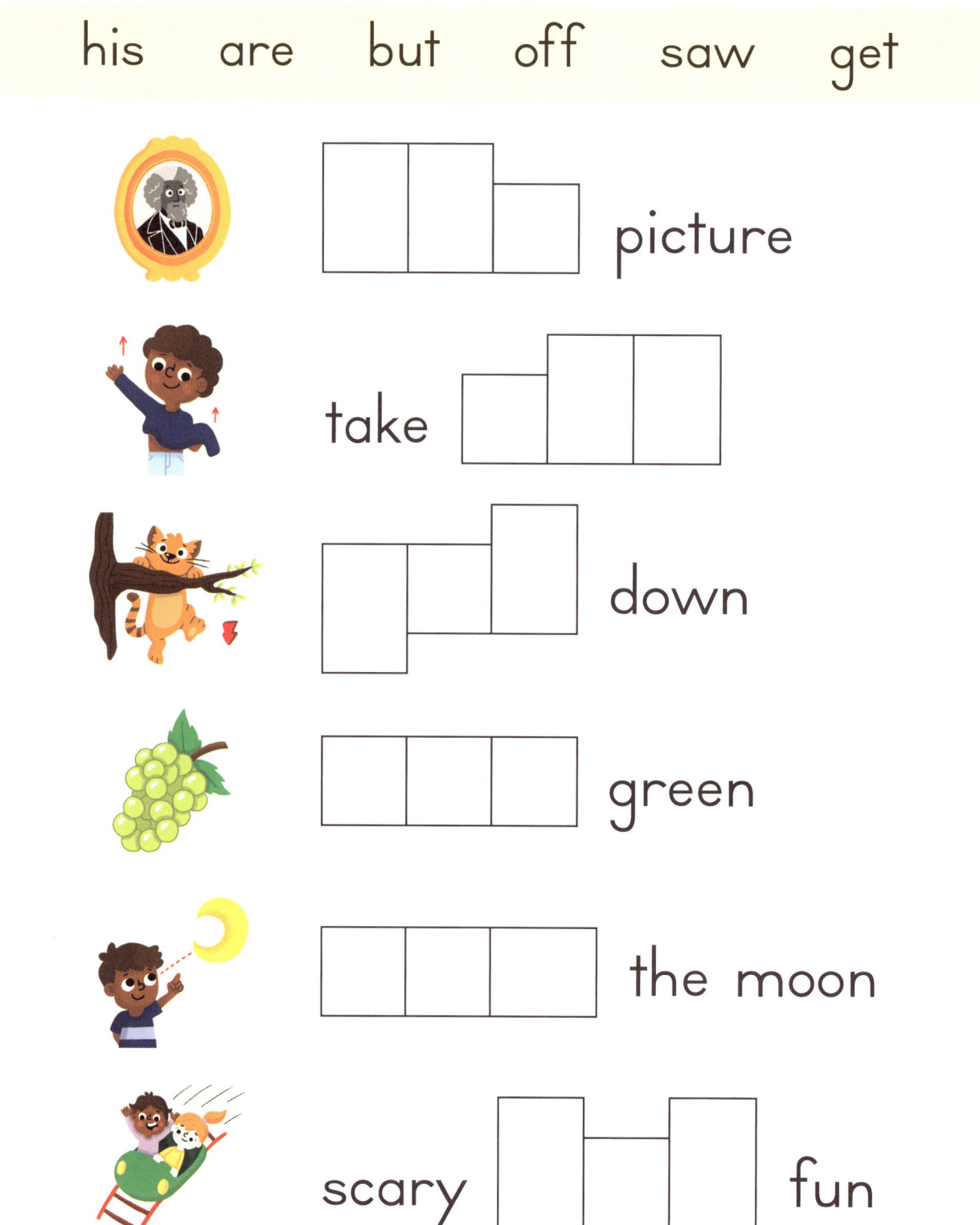

picture

take

down

green

the moon

scary   fun

Our, put, & eat

■ Look at the picture. Then trace and (say) the highlighted word.

our home

our home

our pet

our pet

■ Trace the path from the arrow (➡) to the star (⭐) following the word "our".

our ➡   our   our   are

or   our   oar

ore   our   ⭐ our

■ Look at the picture. Then trace and (say) the highlighted word.

put away

put down

■ Color each crab that has the word "put". Use any color.

Our, put, & eat

■ Look at the picture. Then trace and (say) the highlighted word.

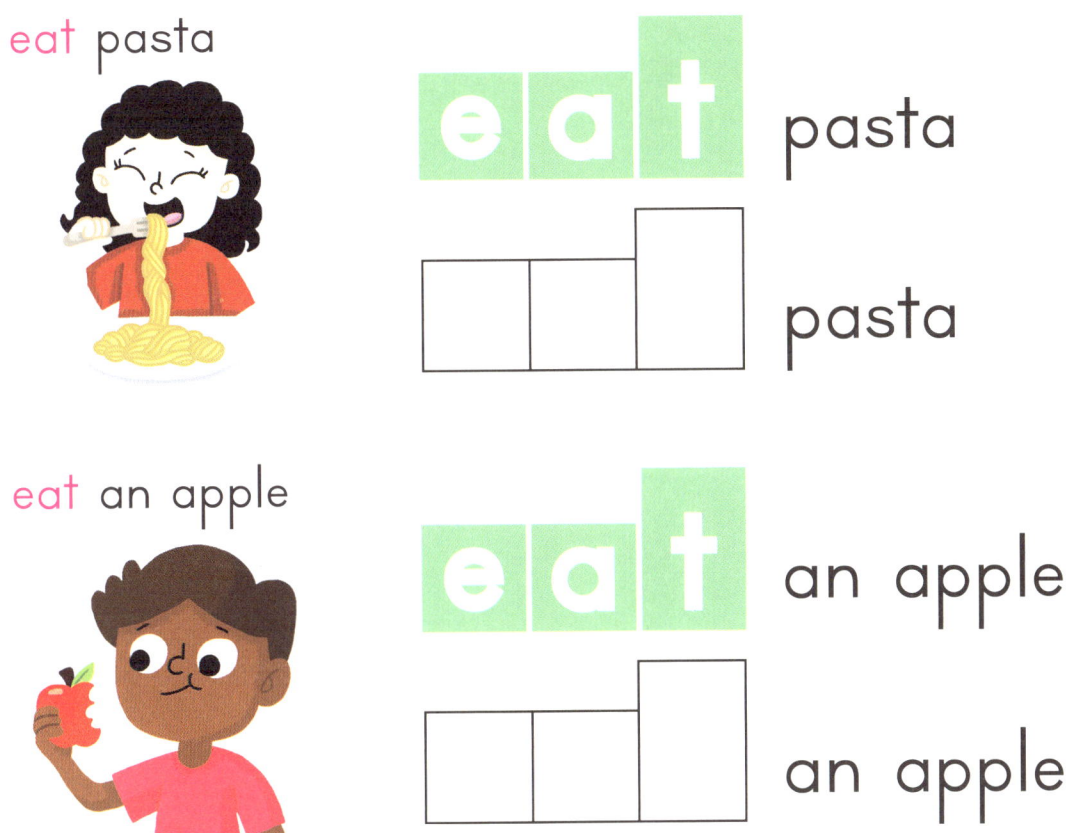

eat pasta

eat pasta

pasta

eat an apple

eat an apple

an apple

■ Find and circle the word "eat". It appears **4** times. It may be written across (➡) or down (⬇).

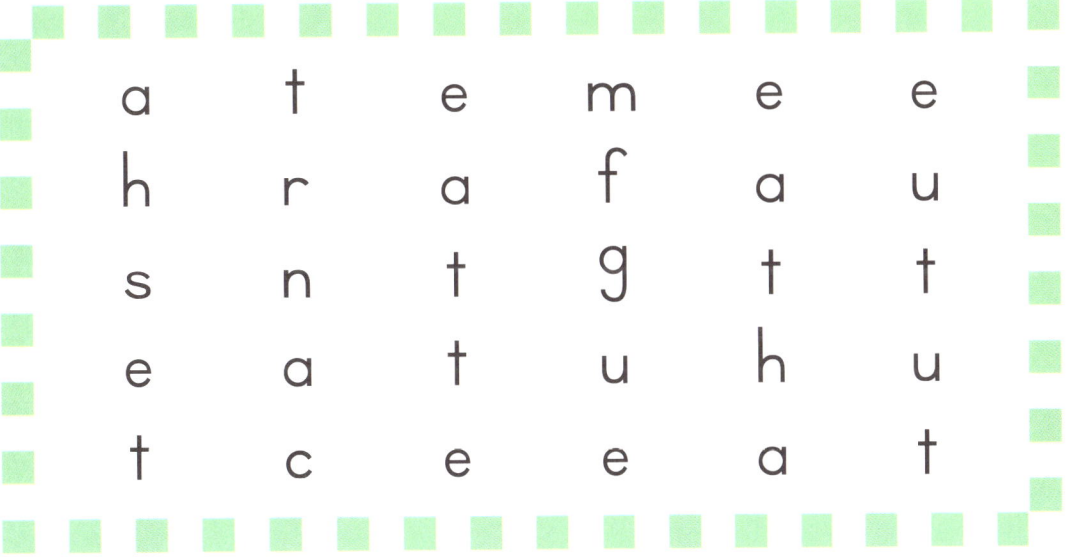

a	t	e	m	e	e
h	r	a	f	a	u
s	n	t	g	t	t
e	a	t	u	h	u
t	c	e	e	a	t

■ Look at the picture. Then trace and write the highlighted word.

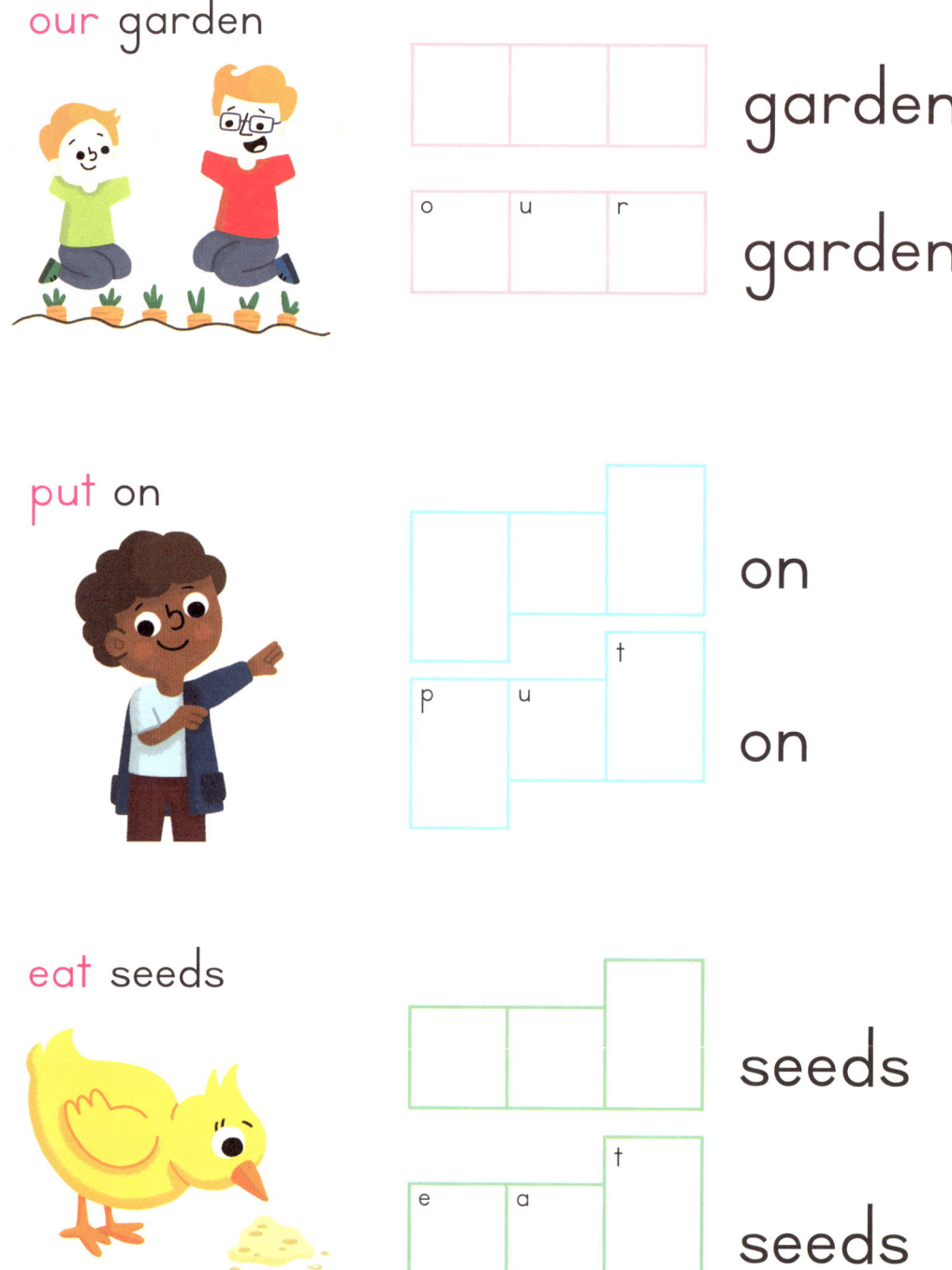

our garden

garden

o u r garden

put on

on

p u t on

eat seeds

seeds

e a t seeds

38

Its, out, & she

■ Look at the picture. Then trace and (say) the highlighted word.

its bed

i t s bed

i t s bed

its petals

i t s petals

i t s petals

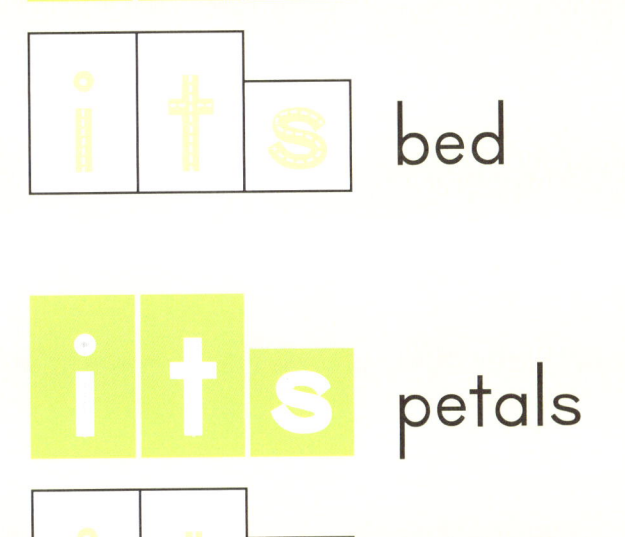

■ Trace the path from the arrow (➡) to the star (★) following the word "its".

its ➡   itt    its   its

        its   its

itz  ils   it's   ★ its

■ Look at the picture. Then trace and (say) the highlighted word.

out the door

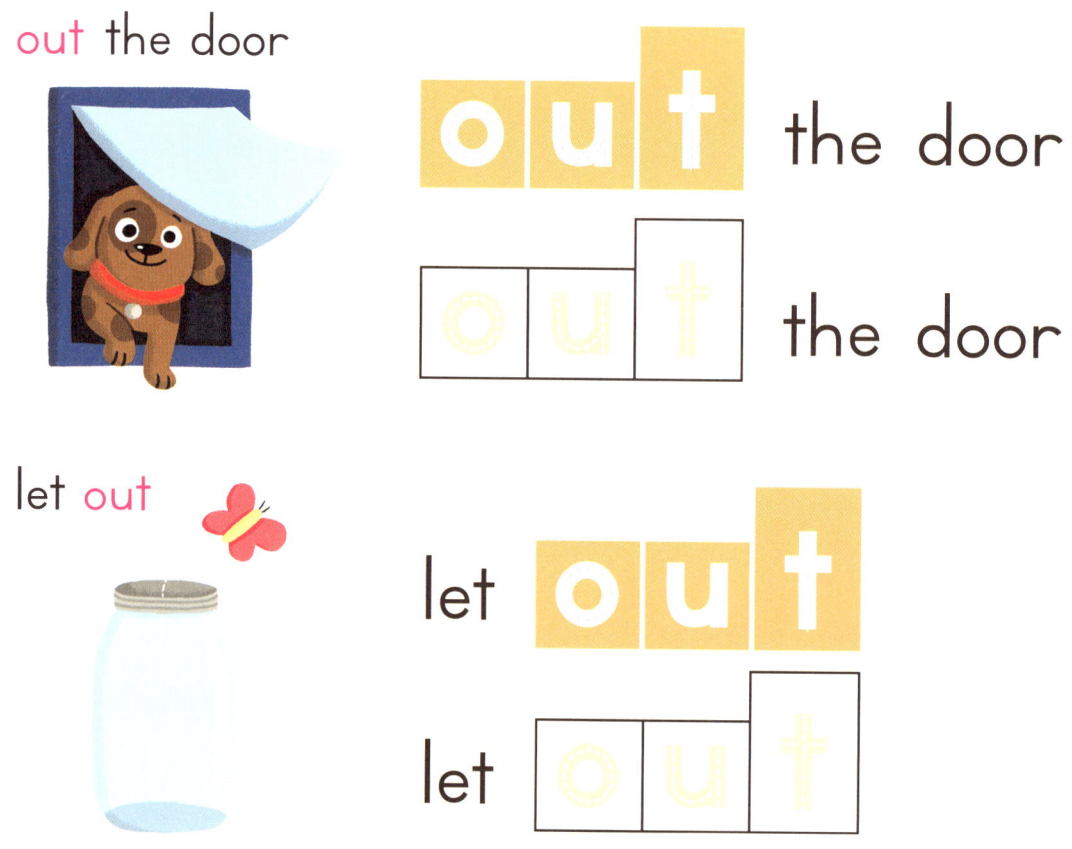

out the door

out the door

let out

let out

let out

■ Color each penguin that has the word "out". Use any color.

39

Its, out, & she

■ Look at the picture. Then trace and (say) the highlighted word.

she sits

she   sits

sits

she roars

she   roars

roars

■ Find and circle the word "she". It appears **4** times. It may be written across (➡) or down (⬇).

z	h	s	h	e	c
h	g	z	s	t	e
e	a	c	s	s	s
s	h	e	h	u	h
o	s	t	e	r	e

■ Look at the picture. Then trace and write the highlighted word.

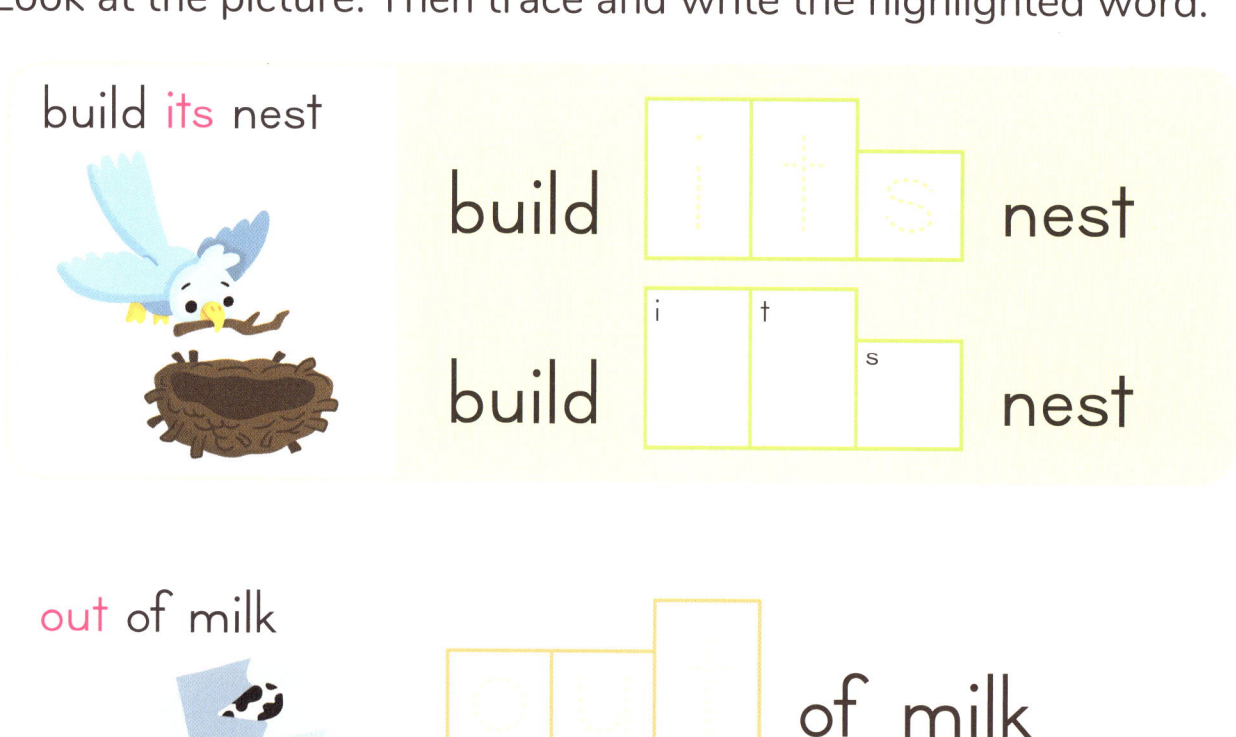

build **its** nest

build i t s nest

build i t s nest

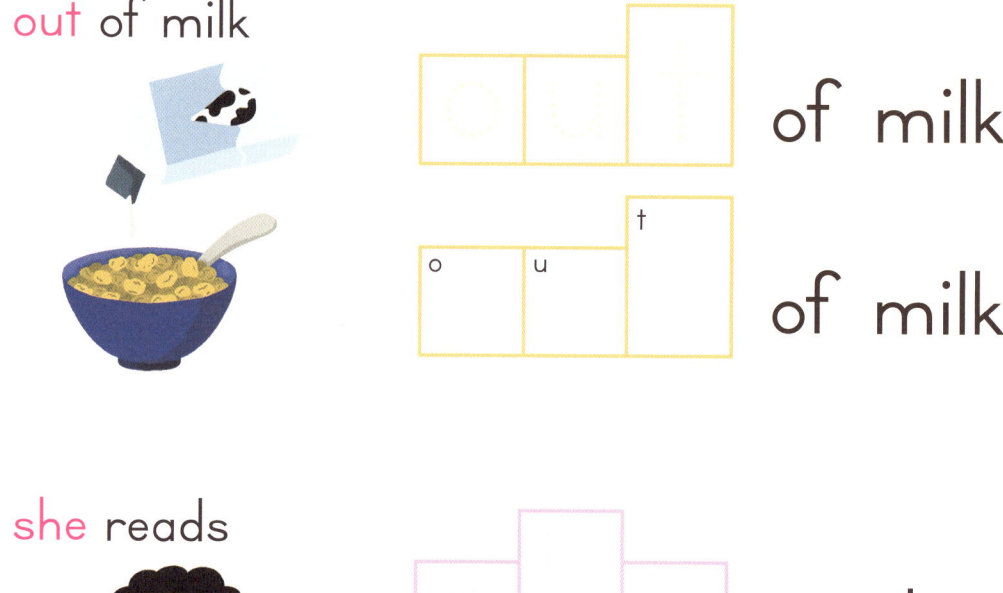

out of milk

o u t of milk

o u t of milk

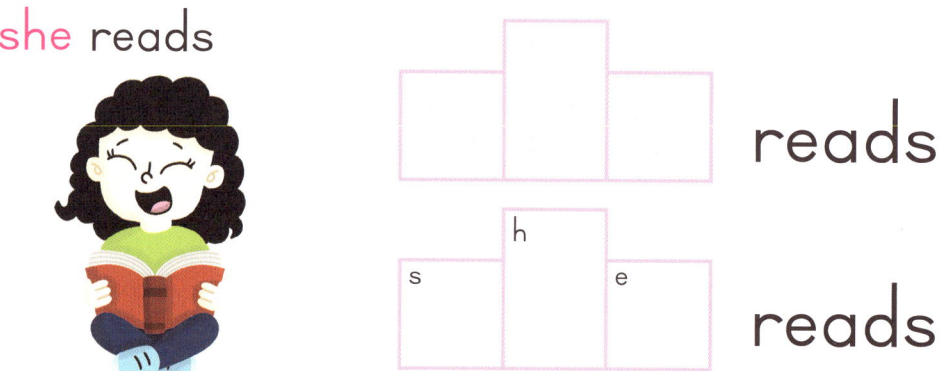

she reads

s h e reads

s h e reads

Review
Our, put, eat, its, out, & she

■ Trace each word. Then match each word with the phrase it is in. Part of the word is hidden.

 put down

 eat pasta

 our pet

 let out

she sits

its petals

79

■ (Say) each word in the word bank. Then fill in the blanks with words from the word bank.

| our | put | eat | its | out | she |

roars

build ____ nest

on

home

an apple

of milk

Own, use, & who

■ Look at the picture. Then trace and (say) the highlighted word.

on my own

on my **own**

on my ⬚⬚⬚

my own idea

my **own** idea

my ⬚⬚⬚ idea

■ Trace the path from the arrow (➡) to the star (⭐) following the word "own".

own ➡   own   owm

oun   own   own   mow

          one   own   ⭐ own

81

■ Look at the picture. Then trace and (say) the highlighted word.

use glue

u s e glue

u s e glue

use scissors

u s e scissors

u s e scissors

■ Color each balloon that has the word "use". Use any color.

Own, use, & who

■ Look at the picture. Then trace and (say) the highlighted word.

who is

who is

is

who was

who was

was

■ Find and circle the word "who". It appears **4** times. It may be written across (➡) or down (⬇).

■ Look at the picture. Then trace and write the highlighted word.

own a pet

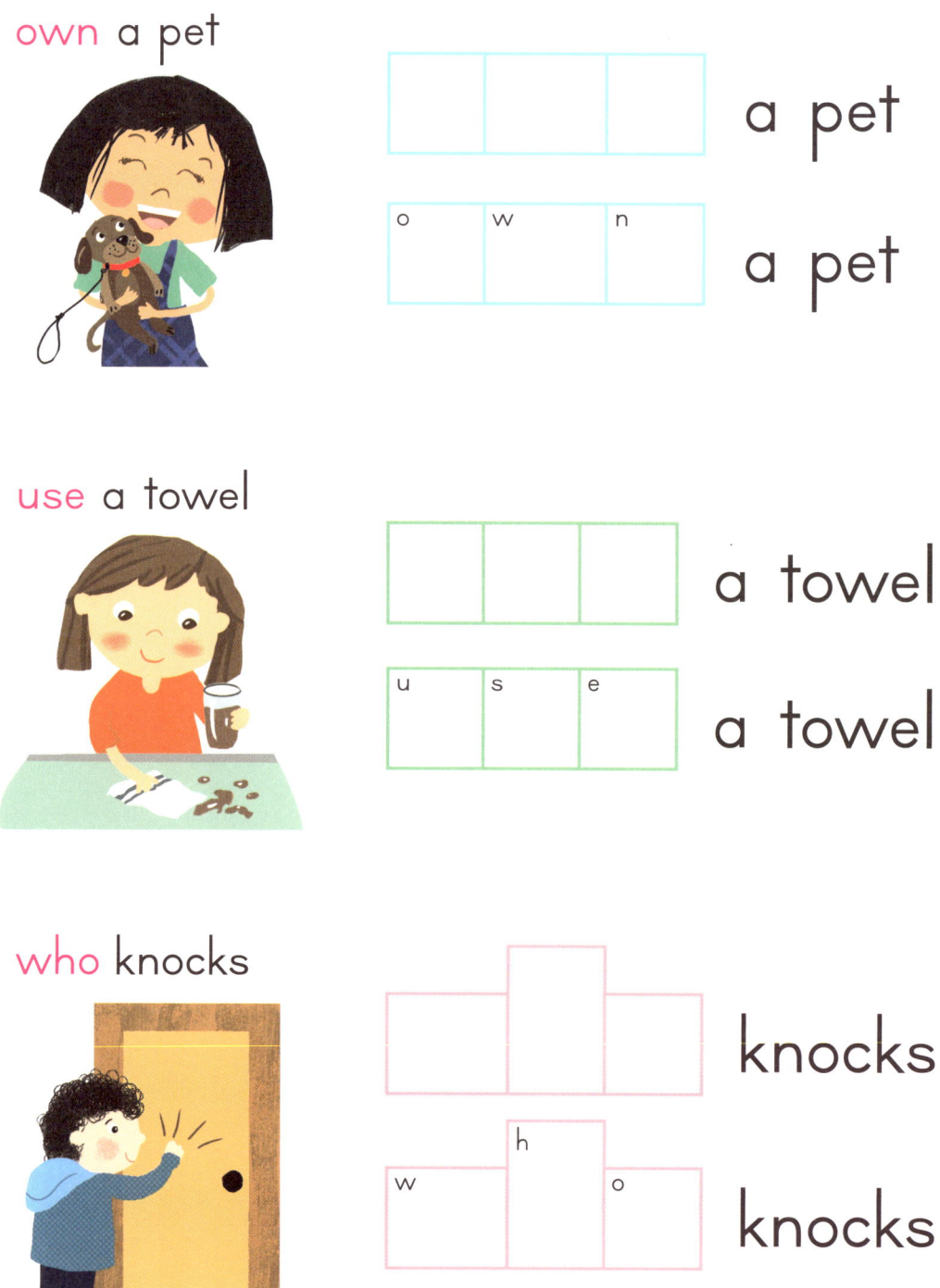

a pet

o	w	n

a pet

use a towel

a towel

u	s	e

a towel

who knocks

knocks

w	h	o

knocks

It's, any, & now

To parents/guardians: In this book, *it's* is always used to start a complete sentence that is concluded with a period. So, here, you will see this word with a capitalized first letter. You can let your child know that, as with most words, whether *it's* is capitalized depends on its use in a sentence.

■ Look at the picture. Then trace and (say) the highlighted word.

It's big.

It's big.

It's small.

It's small.

■ Trace the path from the arrow (➡) to the star (★) following the word "It's"

■ Look at the picture. Then trace and (say) the highlighted word.

any minute

any minute

minute

any seat

any seat

seat

■ Color each flower that has the word "any". Use any color.

It's, any, & *now*

■ Look at the picture. Then trace and (say) the highlighted word.

leave now

leave **now**

leave **now**

start now

start **now**

start **now**

■ Find and circle the word "now". It appears **4** times. It may be written across (➡) or down (⬇).

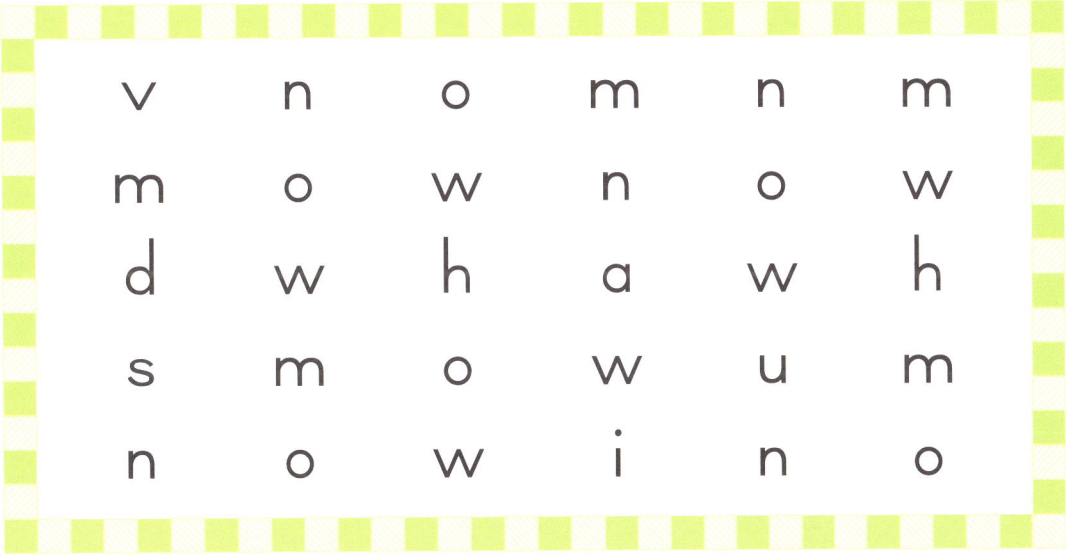

v	n	o	m	n	m
m	o	w	n	o	w
d	w	h	a	w	h
s	m	o	w	u	m
n	o	w	i	n	o

■ Look at the picture. Then trace and write the highlighted word.

It's dark.

I t ' s dark.

I t ' s dark.

any day

day

a n y day

open it now

open it n o w

open it n o w

Review

Own, use, who, it's, any, & now

Name

Date

/ /

To parents/guardians: This is the last section in this workbook. Offer your child lots of praise for completing this book.

■ Trace each word. Then match each word with the phrase or sentence it is in. Part of the word is hidden.

  use glue •

  who is •

 my own idea •

  leave now •

  any seat •

  It's small. •

■ (Say) each word in the word bank. Then fill in the blanks with words from the word bank.

own   use   who   It's   any   now

start

a pet

big.

day

knocks

scissors

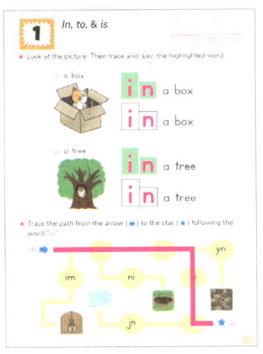

page 1

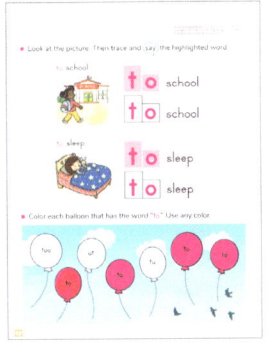

page 2

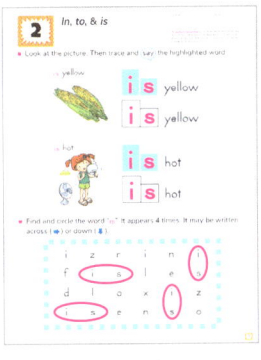

page 3

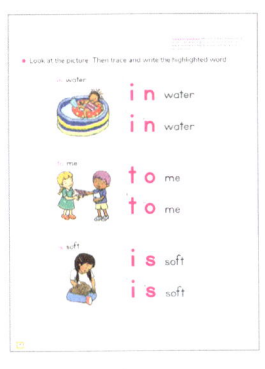

page 4

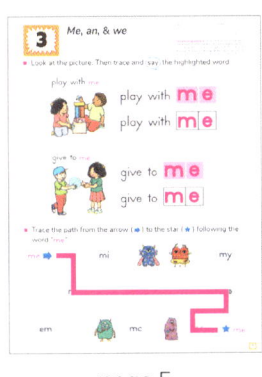

page 5

page 6

page 7

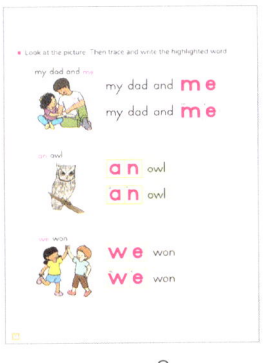

page 8

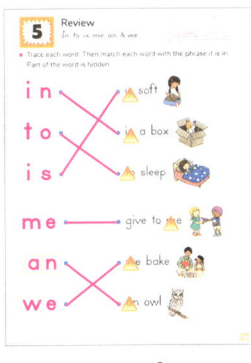

page 9

page 10

page 11

page 12

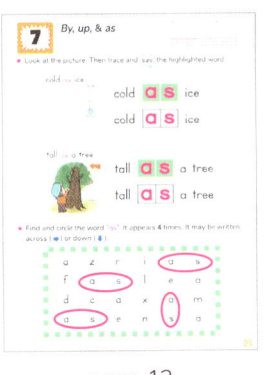

page 13

page 14

page 15

page 16

page 17

page 18

page 19

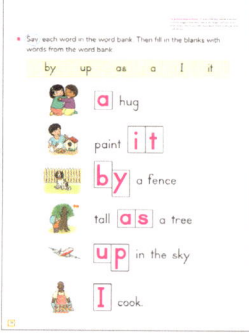

page 20

page 21

page 22

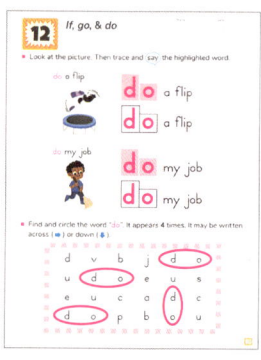

page 23

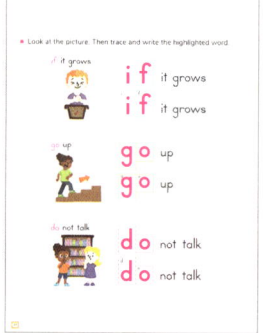

page 24

page 25

page 26

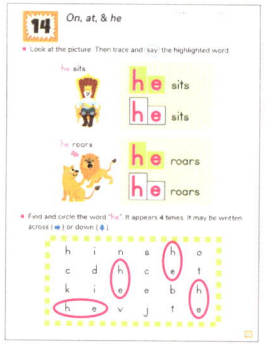

page 27

page 28

page 29

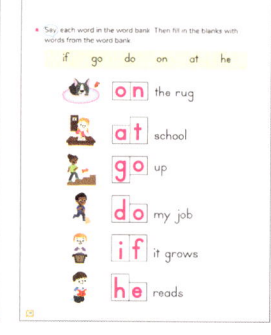

page 30

page 31

page 32

page 33

page 34

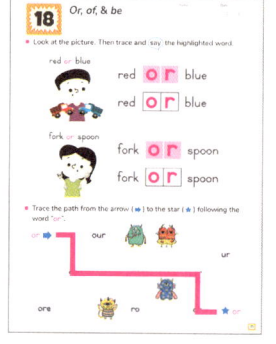

page 35

page 36

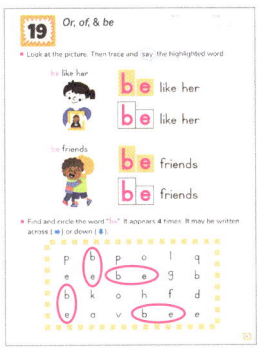

page 37

page 38

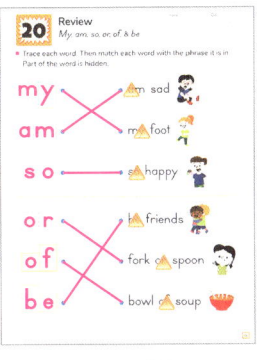

page 39

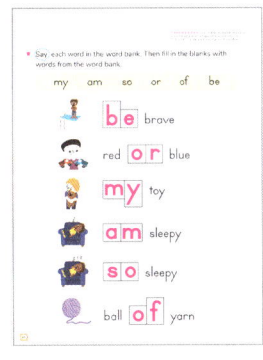

page 40

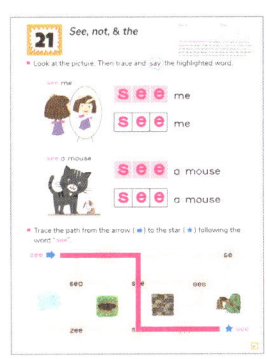

page 41

page 42

page 43

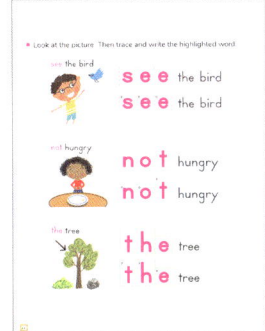

page 44

page 45

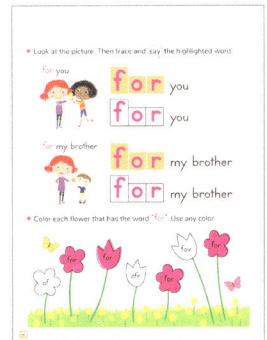

page 46

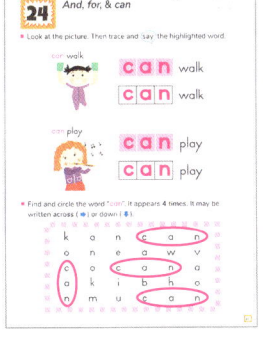

page 47

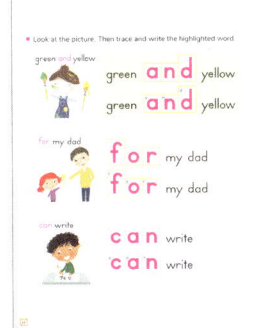

page 48

page 49

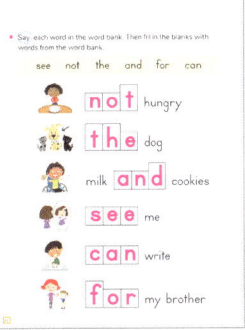

page 50

page 51

page 52

page 53

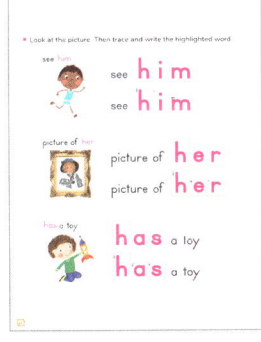

page 54

My Book of Reading Skills: Easy Sight Words Answer Key

page 55

page 56

page 57

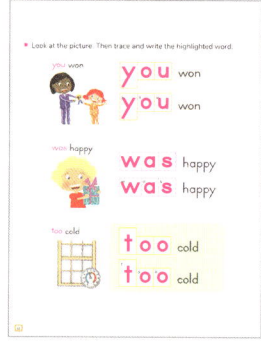
page 58

page 59

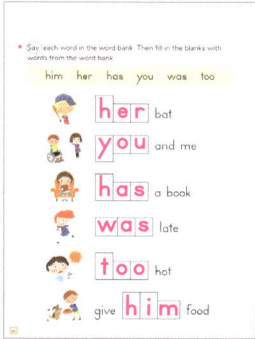
page 60

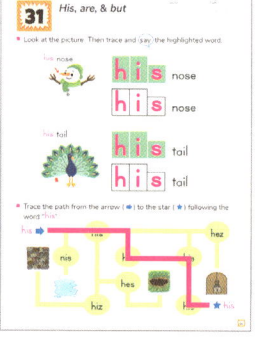
page 61

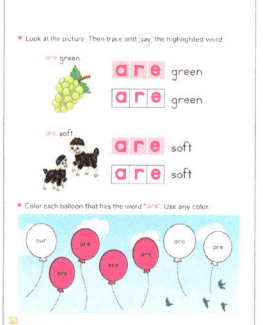
page 62

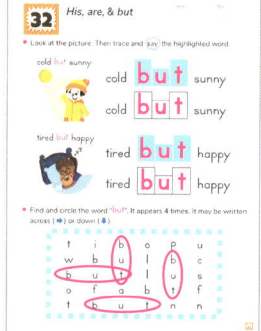
page 63

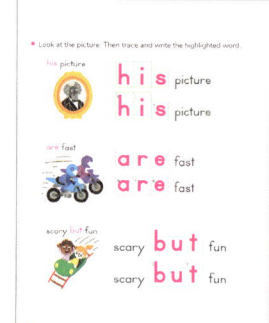
page 64

page 65

page 66

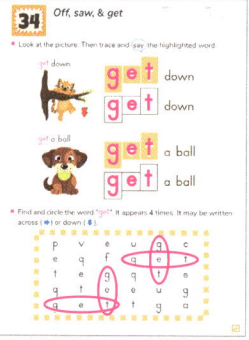
page 67

page 68

page 69

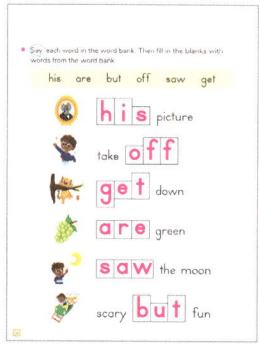
page 70

page 71

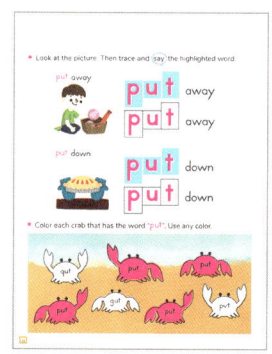
page 72

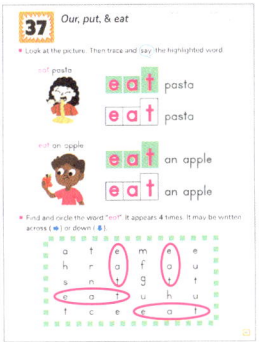

page 73

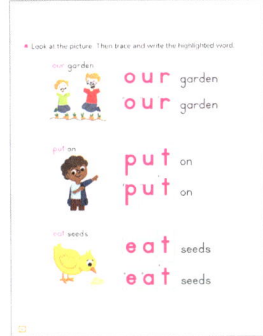

page 74

page 75

page 76

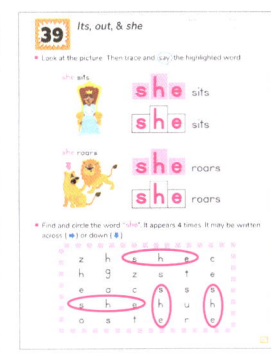

page 77

page 78

page 79

page 80

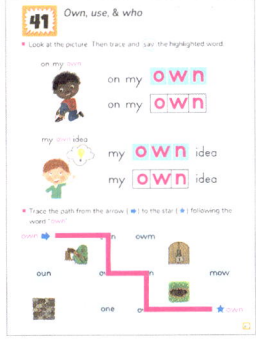

page 81

page 82

page 83

page 84

page 85

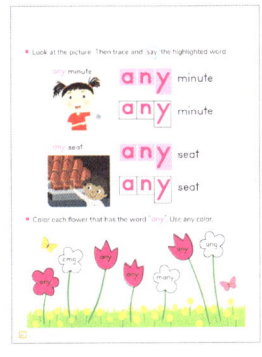

page 86

page 87

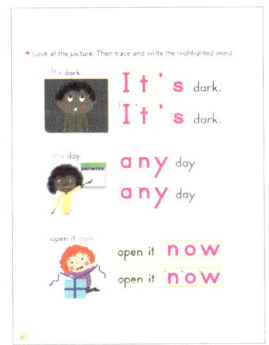

page 88

page 89

page 90

Certificate of Achievement

is hereby congratulated on completing

My Book of Reading Skills: Easy Sight Words

Presented on   , 20

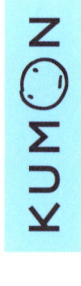

KUM◯N

Parent or guardian